Typical Jenny Morgan or Welsh girl vane

Shamrock's vane. An example of a gate or circular saw vane

Albion's vane

Mermaid's vane

Horsey

Somerton

Martham

Stokesby

Breydon

YARMOUTH

Southtown

y Arms

Gorleston

Herringfleet

Somerleyton

LOWESTOFT

Oulton Broad

D1612717

Trading wherry converted for pleasure trips, c. 1890

Purpose-built pleasure wherry

WHERRIES AND WATERWAYS

WHERRIES AND WATERWAYS

The story of the Norfolk and Suffolk wherry
and the waterways on which it sailed.

by

ROBERT MALSTER

Foreword by Major J. A. Forsythe, T.D.
President of the Norfolk Wherry Trust.

TERENCE DALTON LIMITED

LAVENHAM   SUFFOLK

1986

Published by
TERENCE DALTON LIMITED
ISBN 0 86138 042 8

First Published 1971
Second Impression 1973
Third Impression 1978
Revised Edition 1986

Printed in Great Britain at
The Lavenham Press Limited, Lavenham, Suffolk

Contents

Index of Illustrations

Foreword

by
Major J. A. FORSYTHE, T.D.
President of the Norfolk Wherry Trust

AT ONE TIME it was said that anyone who had not seen a wherry and a windmill had not seen East Anglia. The author of this book once wrote: "The era of the wherry was the era of the windmill. Both used windpower and both grew to be things of beauty whose passing was regretted long after they had disappeared from the Broadland scene. When artists of the Norwich School were painting little skeleton mills and tumbledown boarded windpumps with primitive canvas-covered sails, the wherry was a rather blundering craft with a low-peaked sail. The building of fine brick tower mills with their patent sails, their fantails, and in some cases turbines instead of scoop wheels to raise the water, was undertaken at the same period that some of the finest wherries were produced in riverside yards; sweet-lined, beautiful craft with a fine entry and an easy run, and high-peaked sails hoisted by a geared winch. It was not entirely coincidental that the last trading wherry was launched from Allen's yard at Coltishall in the year that also saw the building of the last Broadland windmill."

And now they are all gone. It is a sobering thought, for a maritime nation, that of all the countless scores of types of small sailing trading and fishing vessels which once abounded on our coasts and on our inland waterways, only a handful remain. In the early thirties there were over two thousand Thames barges in regular trade; today only a score remain, preserved by a handful of enthusiasts. And there is only a single trading wherry, the *Albion*, preserved by a charitable trust, to which the author refers in his last chapter.

Bob Malster was born and brought up in Norwich, once the great centre of the keel and wherry trade. For twenty-five years he has been gathering material and collating information for a definitive book on wherries. With every year that passes, such a task becomes harder; old photographs and records are thrown out and destroyed; half-models and other precious relics are sawn up for firewood. The great wars of the twentieth century, the second of which saw the East Coast ports of Yarmouth and Lowestoft and the city of Norwich heavily bombed, took their toll; and the effects of those wars have certainly not helped the task of any future historian of the East Anglian scene.

It is now almost exactly sixty years since the last trading wherry was built, and over thirty years since the last commercial wherries traded under sail. Despite this lapse of time and all the difficulties which have faced him in his task, the author has amassed a wealth of factual material about the great days of the sailing wherry. He has been fortunate in securing a unique collection of historic photographs, many of which are here published for the first time.

To all lovers of sail and of the many small sailing vessels on which until almost the end of the nineteenth century the vast coastal and inland water-carrying trade of Britain entirely depended, I can wholeheartedly commend this book and the story the author unfolds.

Scoutbush, Hoveton,
Norfolk.

For Andrea and Paul

Introduction and Acknowledgements

THIS BOOK had its genesis nearly a quarter of a century ago, when I would spend afternoons at what I always knew as Hobrough's Dock, though ownership had by then passed to May Gurney & Co. Ltd. On a lucky afternoon I might see *Dora, Bell* or *Elder* coming downriver with another load of mud from the dredger; on even luckier days I would be invited into the big iron boatshed in which *Shamrock, Primus* or another of the firm's motor wherries was undergoing repair, the new strakes, shaped with the adze, held in place with enormous clamps. On summer afternoons during the school holidays cycle rides would give the opportunity of seeing wherries such as *Red Rover, Reindeer, Sundog* and *Beta* used in their old age as houseboats on the Broads; on specially remembered afternoons I saw a pleasure wherry, *Solace, Hathor* or possibly *Dragon,* slipping gently by under the pull of her big white sail.

The day of the sailing trading wherry was already over, though. When in 1949 the Norfolk Wherry Trust was founded to preserve a trading wherry under sail it seemed like an attempt to put the clock back, and many critics voiced the opinion that such an effort was doomed to failure. The fact that *Albion* is still afloat, still travelling the Norfolk waterways under sail, shows that the critics were wrong; the Wherry Trust has succeeded where other similar preservation societies have failed, and long may it continue its excellent work.

One of those who encouraged me in my efforts in those far-off days when I began gathering information about wherries was Mr. Horace Bolingbroke. And but for him this book would never have been written as it has, for it is as much his as mine; he very generously made available to me not only his incomparable notes on the East Anglian waterways, built up over many years, but also his fine collection of photographs which includes even some taken by that pioneer Broads yachtsman and writer, George Christopher Davies, more than eighty years ago.

Much of what I learnt for myself came from Mr. Walter Powley, a retired waterman who willingly enough answered my questions as we sat by the fire on cold winter evenings. I acquired a lot of wherry lore from him. There were others, too, who were happy to spare a little of their time to tell of the old days when sailing wherries were counted by the score and the rivers were alive with trade. Too numerous to mention individually, to them all I owe my thanks.

For information and for the loan of photographs I would wish to thank Major James Forsythe and the Norfolk Wherry Trust, Mr. Humphrey Boardman, Mr. David Cleveland, Mr. Hadingham, Mr. Edward Fisher, Charles Bardswell and others.

Robert Malster,
Ipswich, Suffolk

September, 1971

10

CHAPTER ONE

The Waterways

THE WATERWAYS of east Norfolk and north-east Suffolk must, from very early days, have formed very satisfactory arteries for the trade of the district. Indeed, archaeologists have suggested that in Roman times a fleet of river barges must have existed to carry supplies to certain units of the Roman army performing garrison duty in that outlandish part of Britain and to carry building stone and other materials for the towns of Caistor St. Edmund (Venta Icenorum) and what is now known as Caister-by-Yarmouth. In the valley of the Tas near the site of Venta Icenorum have been found remains of what may be a Roman wharf, and river craft of a somewhat later date have been discovered on the shores of the now non-existent estuary near Yarmouth.

When the broads were being formed by peat diggings in the Middle Ages the ecclesiastical establishments of the area were noting, in their accounts, payments for the carriage of turves, presumably by square-sailed keels not unlike those which can be seen in Thomas Cleer's map of Norwich, drawn in 1696, and similar topographical publications.

Wherry traffic, in the nineteenth century, carried the merchandise and manufactures of Norwich to the sea at Yarmouth and distributed the cargoes of sea-going ships from that port to Norwich and to many other towns and villages throughout the area; up the Waveney to Beccles and Bungay; up the Chet to Loddon; along the Bure and its tributaries to Aylsham, North Walsham and many another place which, before the coming of the internal combustion engine, must have been almost cut off, except by river.

Every village had its staithe, and nineteenth-century property advertisements show how much local trade and commerce depended on the rivers for transport; time and again one reads in the auctioneers' announcements, in such local newspapers as the *Norwich Mercury* and the *Norfolk Chronicle,* phrases such as "very convenient for water carriage" or "close by the navigable river to Yarmouth". The smaller wherries even penetrated to such places as Waxham and Palling, which were reached by the New Cut, a narrow dyke almost four miles long leading northwards and north-westwards from Horsey Mere. Owing to the shallowness of the Cut wherries would sometimes tow a reed barge into which they could unload part of their cargo should they "run out of water".

Though locks were used on the upper reaches of the Bure, Ant and Waveney, the navigation of the river from Yarmouth to Norwich was never dependent on locks or staunches, although dredging became necessary, at any rate when the size of the wherries using the river increased. Suggestions for locks and barrages have been made from time to time, one such idea being discussed in 1838. A civil engineer, Mr. George Edwards, then reported that he was of the opinion that "the river Wensum from the Foundry Bridge to the New Mills"—the section just below the head of navigation within the City of Norwich—"may be deepened to an efficient depth by dredging, at a very much less expense than by building a lock".

The Norwich River, as the watermen called the Yare and its tributary the Wensum which flowed up to the heart of Norwich, carried the major part of the city's trade in the years before the coming of the railways. In the early part of the eighteenth century Norwich was said to rank in wealth and trade only after London and Bristol, and a great part of its trade was waterborne. In 1808 it was remarked that "Norwich adds much to the trade of Yarmouth, by the importation of about 40,000 chaldrons of coals yearly, wine, fish, oil, Irish yarn, and all heavy goods, which come to it from thence by the river Yare; and, in peace, the exportation of its manufactures to Russia, Germany, Holland, Denmark, Norway, Spain, Portugal, Italy &c."

Yet all these cargoes, both incoming and outgoing, had to be transhipped in Yarmouth harbour, for only the very smallest of sea-going vessels could have followed the keels and wherries up the Yare to the city.

The early nineteenth century was a time of great engineering activity, of expansion and development, and the methods that had been good enough for men's grandfathers were no longer to be tolerated by the merchants and businessmen of the city of Norwich. They found the necessity for transhipping goods at Yarmouth both inconvenient and irksome, particularly when Yarmouth bar was found to present an obstacle to the use of the larger vessels being introduced into the merchant fleet at that time.

So it was that a group of Norwich businessmen, tired of the hold-ups and exasperations of transhipping goods from sea-going vessels to keels and wherries and vice-versa, decided to make the river navigable for sea-going vessels right up to the city. William Cubitt, the Norfolk-born civil engineer then working in Ipswich and later knighted for undertaking some of the construction work in connection with the Great Exhibition of 1851, was engaged to carry out a survey and draw up a plan for the navigation in 1814.

His first scheme was a relatively simple one, to dredge the river where necessary and to construct a cut along the south side of Breydon water, the large shallow lake formed at the confluence of the Yare and Waveney. He expected that this could be done for a little over £35,000.

Yarmouth, jealous of its position as an *entrepôt,* did its best to frustrate the efforts of the Norwich merchants, and in 1820 Cubitt produced an alternative proposal for making a new outlet to the sea at Lowestoft. Thomas Telford, an even more famous engineer, reported two years later that Cubitt's schemes were feasible, though he estimated that the original proposal, to make the river navigable by cutting a channel to the south of Breydon, would cost £13,000 more than Cubitt had reckoned.

Just inside the city walls at Norwich. King Street, which runs along the back of the buildings seen here, was a watermen's quarter in the old days.

"I am led to hope for the desirable co-operation of Yarmouth and Norwich, because, as an Engineer, I can foresee no injury to the Harbour or Port of Yarmouth, from the New River Channel", Telford reported. And another engineer, James Walker, reporting to Yarmouth Corporation in 1826, remarked: "The general result of all my consideration is, that the natural Port of Norwich is by Yarmouth, to separate them, were it possible, would be injurious to both, and both parties are, I am convinced, blind to their own interests if they either desire a separation or refuse to each other those facilities which each has the means of offering to the other..."

In spite of such advice, or perhaps because of it, the Yarmouth people offered strong and continued opposition to any plan for making the river navigable for sea-going ships. Yarmouth received support from the proprietors of the North Walsham and Dilham Canal and the Aylsham Navigation. They feared the plans of the Norwich merchants would divert traffic from Yarmouth to Lowestoft and would lead to the neglect of Breydon and consequently to the injury of the navigation of the Bure and Ant.

The "Norwich a Port" party, foremost among whom was a city alderman and maltster, Crisp Brown, were undeterred by the assurance that the Corporation of Yarmouth would do everything in their power to oppose an undertaking "which was

13

pregnant with the most ruinous consequences to the interests of the town and neighbour-hood" and a subscription was opened in 1822.

Evidence given before a Committee of the House of Commons, during the session of 1826, is interesting as showing the state of mind of some of the parties involved. While the masters of several Leith and Berwick smacks were called by the promoters to say how useful a new harbour at Lowestoft would be to those taking part in the coasting trade, the evidence against the Bill included that of a Yarmouth pilot who said he was sure the proposed pier would cause a bar to build up and stop up Lowestoft Roads altogether.

Yarmouth harbour-master John Bracey, arguing that the cost of towing vessels up to Norwich would be prohibitive, showed an inability to prophesy accurately when he remarked: "They would track them up by those steamboats while they last —but they are going out."

The defeat of the Norwich and Lowestoft Navigation Bill in 1826 gave rise to great rejoicing at Yarmouth, but it was Norwich that celebrated the following year when a new Bill passed safely through all its Parliamentary stages. *The Times* coach by

A laden wherry in the Wensum in the heart of Norwich.

A share certificate of the Company of Proprietors of the Norwich and Lowestoft Navigation
1827.
Norfolk Nautical Society

which the promoters had travelled from London was met at Harford Bridges by a procession, and was dragged in triumph through the city after the horses had been removed at St. Stephen's Gates. Wooden palings and watch boxes fed the celebration bonfire in Norwich market place and, when the ringleaders of the mob were lodged in clink, their comrades rescued them and added the clink doors to the fire.

Cubitt's idea was to widen and deepen that part of the river between Foundry and Carrow bridges at Norwich; dredge the river to a minimum of 12 feet to Low Street, near Reedham; and from there he proposed to excavate a 2½-mile cut linking the Yare with the Waveney. Little or nothing would need to be done to the Waveney, but Oulton Dyke would have to be dredged and straightened and a channel would need to be dredged across Oulton Broad.

Perhaps the biggest and most enterprising part of the scheme was the construction of a new harbour just to the south of the little fishing village of Lowestoft. "I propose to enter the sea by a cut from Lake Lothing at an oblique angle to the beach, pointing northward towards Lowestoft Ness, very nearly in the direction of the floating light" (the lightship placed in the Stanford Channel not many years before). "Between Lake Lothing and the cut there will be gates to keep the water in Lake Lothing; and then the means of opening those gates to let out the water into the sea with great velocity"— that was the way Cubitt planned to prevent the accumulation of the bar promised by the Yarmouth denigrators of his scheme. There was also to be a lock between Lake Lothing and Oulton Broad, where one still exists. Cubitt estimated that the whole of the works could be carried out for £100,000, although six years earlier he had estimated the cost at £87,000 including a sum for contingencies—inflation is no new thing.

Mr. Crisp Brown dug the first spadeful of earth when the work of excavation began in the autumn of 1827, and in 1832 the New Cut was opened from the Yare to the Waveney to link Norwich with the new harbour. The first seaborne vessel to sail from London to Norwich direct, the 120-ton steam packet *Thames,* must have used the shallow channel over Breydon, because it is recorded that she arrived at Carrow Bridge in May, 1828, after a 28-hour voyage. Lowestoft harbour was not completed until some three years afterwards.

The date on which Norwich is traditionally said to have become a port was September 30th, 1833, when the *City of Norwich* and the *Squire,* the first vessels to enter the Norwich River direct from the sea by way of the New Cut, were towed upriver to be met by the Mayor of Norwich. Sea-going ships had been to Norwich before— indeed the 61-ton sloop *Squire* had been built at Carrow by Thomas Batley in 1831, the second sea-going vessel to be "raised" on his yard—but that day was remembered ever after as the day on which Norwich became a port.

With the completion of the New Cut and Lowestoft harbour Yarmouth must have been seen to have lost the battle to retain the trade of Norwich. But when arrangements were made for the *s.s. Jarrow* to tow the *City of Norwich* and the *Squire* from Lowestoft to Norwich the Yarmouth harbour officials staged a delaying action, refusing to open the Haven Bridge so that the *Jarrow* could pass through on her way to Lowestoft because, they said, it was a Sunday. Eventually Capt. Wilkinson of the *Jarrow* unbolted part of the funnel and squeezed his vessel under the bridge, but he lost the tide and had to wait on Breydon for the next high water. One wonders why he did not solve his problem by making the 12-mile sea passage to Lowestoft.

Consternation was caused at Lowestoft, where the *Susanna,* another small steamer, was engaged to tow the two traders against a headwind towards the city. Her 7 h.p. engine proved hardly equal to the task and it was not until the *Jarrow* met the little procession at Haddiscoe that any real progress was made. Even then the difficulties had not all been met for when, about eight miles below Norwich, the crew of the *Susanna* learned that the *Jarrow* and the *City of Norwich* were to be given the honour of being the first to reach the city they cast off the towrope. A young seaman, the son of

Capt. Allerton of the *City of Norwich,* fell from his small boat and was drowned as he carried a new towrope to the *Squire*.

Mr. Crisp Brown had not lived to see the fulfilment of his dream, for he had died on board the *Lyra* while on an Atlantic voyage, taken for the benefit of his health, in 1830.

Both the *Squire* and her consort, the 74-ton schooner *City of Norwich,* built at Lowestoft by John Korff in 1832, were owned by the London, Lowestoft, Norwich and Beccles Shipping and Trading Company, which advertised later in 1833 the establishment of a regular weekly service between London and Norwich. The *Squire* was one of the first vessels owned by the company, which bought the schooner *Sally* from King's Lynn and a second schooner, the *Orion,* in 1831. Thomas Branford built the 80-ton schooners *Lowestoft Merchant* and *Norwich Trader* at Yarmouth for the company in 1834, in which year the *Orion* was sold to Wells and replaced by the schooner *Sarah,* built at Wells the previous year. The company also owned another *Sarah,* a sloop, and the Wells-built sloop *Ocean,* which was bought in 1838. The trustees of the company were all Lowestoft men.

Preparing to warp a small brig into a fresh berth at Yarmouth, with wherries lying at the quay in the background. It was vessels of about this size which traded to Norwich.

Bishop's Bridge, Norwich, a medieval structure which at one time had a tower on one of the piers. Like other old bridges, it proved something of an obstacle to navigation, and also on occasion to floodwater. The wherry is lying alongside a tannery.

These vessels trading to Norwich in the early days of the navigation were very small craft, the *Squire* having a length of only 58 ft. and a beam of 15 ft. 9 in. The schooners were little bigger, the *Sally,* built in 1826, being only 57 ft. 8 in. long with a breadth of 18 ft. 3 in. and a depth of 9 ft. 10 in. She was 80 tons old measurement against the *Squire's* 61 tons.

Ambitious plans for docks at Norwich never reached fruition and only the *Clarence Harbour* public house, overlooking the Norwich Thorpe railway yards where the docks were to have been, bore witness to the scheme in later years. Although £100,000 had been sunk in the work, little permanent benefit was derived by the city.

Shifting sands blocked the lock at the entrance to Lowestoft harbour, in spite of Cubitt's plans to flush away the accretion by occasionally opening the gates, while easterly winds and accompanying heavy seas undermined the harbour works, and the navigation of the river was all but stopped. When the government, unable to obtain repayment of the money advanced to the proprietors of the Navigation, foreclosed in 1842 the harbour was bought by a number of Lowestoft men. They sold it two years later to Sir Samuel Morton Peto, who may, with some justification, claim to be one of the greatest benefactors Lowestoft has ever had. The Act he obtained in 1845 was not only for the improvement of the harbour but also for the building of a railway. Thus began the long connection between Lowestoft harbour and the railway companies, something which has not always been entirely to the advantage of the harbour.

The rebuilding of the harbour seems to have rejuvenated the shipping trade of Norwich. In 1846 one reads of a 70-ton Dutch-built Norwich-owned vessel bringing coal to the city and of no fewer than 18 vessels arriving with cargoes in one week.

In 1849 their Lordships of the Admiralty intimated that they would assent to the Great Yarmouth Haven, Bridge and Navigation Bill subject to certain conditions. These included a clause compelling the Yarmouth Haven Commissioners, who had a year or so earlier opposed a new move to improve the navigation of the River Yare in order to bring ships to Norwich by way of Yarmouth, to deepen the channel over Breydon and across Burgh Flats to not less than 10 feet at low water. It was this ridge which had proved the main obstacle all along. The dredging of a channel through the shallows would have opened the river to deep-draught vessels and have made the Lowestoft navigation unnecessary. Only the opposition of Yarmouth had prevented this relatively inexpensive work being carried out in the 1820s.

The navigation from Lowestoft to Norwich was lightly used for many years, but after the 1850s the story of Lowestoft harbour became more closely linked with the development of local railways than with the Norwich navigation and when small coasting steamers and motor vessels began to trade to Norwich in the 1920s it was at Yarmouth that they began their inland voyaging.

These schemes for making Norwich a port stopped short at Foundry Bridge, the lowest but one of the several bridges crossing the River Wensum. Cargoes carried up to the city by sea-going vessels had still to be unloaded or transhipped below this bridge. Even if the vessels that brought them had lowering masts the depth of water was insufficient for them to penetrate into the heart of the city. Dredging to any extent was impracticable as the foundations of buildings along the banks would be undermined.

Bishop's Bridge, a medieval stone bridge a few hundred yards upstream, had arches which were so low and narrow that nothing but a keel or wherry could negotiate even the central arch. Indeed, it was an obstacle even to the larger wherries, and when the 80-ton *Wonder,* the largest wherry built, delivered a freight of 84 tons of gas coal to Norwich she was unable to return under Bishop's Bridge after being unloaded. A large number of men had to be commissioned to stand on the hatches in order to weigh the wherry down and thus reduce the freeboard. Eventually she did squeeze through, but several men were injured when the hatches gave way and they fell into the hold.

The position at Norwich was made worse by alterations to the mouth of Yarmouth haven in 1826-27 which resulted in a lowering of the water level in the city by, it is said, 18 inches or 2 foot. Some idea of the extraordinary difficulties of navigation in the Norwich section of the river may be gained from a report made to Yarmouth Haven Commissioners in 1838 by Mr. George Edwards. He found that the narrowest part of the river was only 25 feet wide, and had this comment to make:

"The name which this part of the river has obtained (Hell Hole) is scarcely severe enough to convey a just idea of the excessive nuisance that here exists to the navigation, it is a disgrace to the city."

There was then a considerable amount of business being carried on in this part, and craft even lay there to retail coal. When a wherry needed to pass, all the craft lying in the narrow section had to drop down to the wider part of the river. Afterwards they had to heave back to their former berths, a difficult and time-wasting exercise because of the strong current.

Even at the beginning of the present century the situation at Norwich was a most difficult one. The river was very narrow and, in winter especially, the ebb tide ran very hard, backed up with fresh water coming down through the New Mills. Wherries sometimes took cargoes right up into the pool at the New Mills, and when a large amount of water was let through, as it often was after heavy rain, they had to be moved to avoid being swamped.

It was, therefore, a difficult job to get a laden wherry up through the city bridges. Sail was useless, and quants made little progress against the swirling current; thus it was usual to run a line out to a convenient post and to haul the wherry ahead either by using the winch or, when the mast was down and the winch swung aside and out of action, by using a tackle employing the sheet blocks. Once the *Tiger's* winch was strained in "bowsing" her in that way.

There was an occasion when it took a whole day to move two wherries about a quarter of a mile from the *Adam and Eve,* a little old public house tucked away in a corner near the gasworks, up to Quayside and to Jewson's timberyard just above Fye Bridge. In the 1830s it was not unknown for a wherry to take three days to get the mile and a half from Bishop's Bridge up to the New Mills.

"Yachting cruise, July and August 1884" is pencilled on the back of this photograph taken by G. Christopher Davies near Oulton Dyke. The ketch-rigged billy-boy, with her squares'l yard cockbilled, is on her way up the Waveney to Beccles.

Such work as this needed the services of more than the two men who ordinarily worked a wherry. The necessary help was often given by Billy Lancaster, who lived in King Street near the Ferry Inn. He owned a boat in which he would row down to Trowse Eye, the confluence of Yare and Wensum, when he knew there were wherries on the way up. Billy was not above five feet tall, and for that reason was nicknamed "Flea" by the waterside fraternity.

For a fee of a shilling and a pint o' beer, that cost tuppence, he would steer the wherry through the bridges while the wherrymen quanted, one on each side. His little boat came in useful for taking out a line when it became necessary to bowse a heavily laden wherry through the bridges.

Besides "Flea" there were also two men who in winter would help the wherrymen to quant—that meant two quants at work on each side. Their fee for this service was half a crown each.

Whatever the feelings at Yarmouth, the people of Beccles had been in favour of the Norwich plans to construct a ship canal to Norwich by way of a harbour at Lowestoft. This was because the new harbour provided a short way to the sea down the Waveney from Beccles. In 1831 the Corporation of Beccles and other commissioners obtained an Act for deepening the river from Beccles to its meeting with the Norwich and Lowestoft Navigation, but this attempt at improving the town's maritime trade proved unprofitable. Heavy port dues caused much of the traffic to be carried on still in wherries from Yarmouth, and eventually the railway took practically all the trade.

Billy-boys like the ketch-rigged *Yarborough*, of Lowestoft, from which a boy was lost overboard in the river as she sailed downriver with a cargo of malt and peas in 1859, continued trading to Beccles for many years. There were still auxiliary barges bringing wheat to the Beccles mills in the 1950s. Shipping lists in 18th-century newspapers show that for a time at least Beccles was quite a busy minor port, even if it suffered from the problems of most river ports.

The Rochester barge *Cabby* brought the first cargo for 14 years to the Corporation Quay in 1954. She was followed by other vessels: some made the journey up the Yare to Reedham and along the New Cut and others squeezed through the lock from Lowestoft harbour. The first to take the latter course was the *George and Eliza,* a little Rochester barge which sank off West Mersea a few years later after striking the submerged wreck of a wartime concrete lighter.

Not all barges could get through Mutford lock into Oulton Broad. When the barge *Phoenician* was built at Sittingbourne in 1922 a condition of the contract was that she had to be of the maximum possible size to pass through the lock to enable her to take part in the trade up to Beccles. This was effected by rounding her quarters in sharply to a transom somewhat narrower than usual to enable the lock gates to close clear of her. She had an overall length of 84 foot 1 inch and a beam of 20 foot 8 inches.

Vessels such as that could go no further than Beccles bridge, but wherries regularly traded to Bungay, where a number of such craft were built. To reach Bungay they passed through locks at Shipmeadow, also known as Geldeston, Ellingham and Wainford.

When the Waveney was first made navigable to Bungay is unknown, for although an Act was passed in 1670 for making the river navigable it is said to have been navigable in former times for lighters, keels and other boats of considerable burthen. It was at that time so obstructed as to be unnavigable above Beccles, causing great poverty to the inhabitants of the surrounding district. The result of the reopening of the river seems to have been a great improvement in the trade of Bungay, which for many years depended largely on the river for its transport services.

Doubtless the river played a very large part in aiding Matthias Kerrison, the Bungay merchant, to make his fortune during the French wars. He owned the navigation for more than 40 years, and when he died in 1827 he left property worth only a little less than a million pounds.

Towards the end of the last century the navigation passed into the hands of W.D. & A.E. Walker, the Bungay maltsters and merchants, who were the owners of a fleet of wherries, some of them built at Bungay staithe at their private yard. They were succeeded by Watney, Combe, Reid & Co. in 1919, but by then the river trade was in its last decline. The navigation was closed in 1934.

Among the other small country towns served by river transport was Loddon, at the head of navigation of the Chet, a tributary of the Yare just above Reedham. Little more than three miles of navigable water, the Chet was narrow and winding and the navigable section terminated in a small basin just below the little weather-boarded water mill standing at the side of the Norwich-Lowestoft road.

The basin today has been dredged out for the benefit of the motor cruisers based at the boatyards which have sprung up in recent years. Even so it is difficult to imagine it as it was when Woods, Sadd, Moore & Co. owned the iron wherries *Uranus, Vega* and *Sirius* and the wooden wherries *Orion* and *Beniamin,* which used to carry much of the firm's corn and seed between Loddon and Norwich, Yarmouth, Lowestoft and other places. This firm, founded in 1884 by Mr. Arthur Sadd, moved its head office to Norwich in 1919 but continued to own wherries until 1932.

Some idea of what it was like in those days can be judged from what Dr. P. H. Emerson found in 1890 when he took his little wherry, the *Maid of the Mist,* formerly the trader *Little Spark,* up to Loddon on Guy Fawkes' Night:

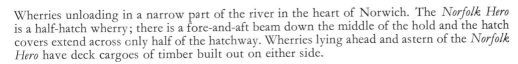

Wherries unloading in a narrow part of the river in the heart of Norwich. The *Norfolk Hero* is a half-hatch wherry; there is a fore-and-aft beam down the middle of the hold and the hatch covers extend across only half of the hatchway. Wherries lying ahead and astern of the *Norfolk Hero* have deck cargoes of timber built out on either side.

Towards night the tide came up, the wind went down, and the rain turned to a cold drizzle. Our ship gradually righted itself, and a few minutes before nine we heard a voice shouting—

"Oh! ho! Maid of the Mist ahoy."

We turned out, and found some wherries astern who wanted to pass to the granary. I took our cabin lamp and stood it on deck, lighting up the dark little basin on that drizzly November night. The mud barge was moored under some dripping trees, and a great wherry came up and slid between us, the crew in dripping oilies chaffing.

"What! going to haul the trawl, Old Robert," said one.

Then another—

"Minds me of coming into harbour fishin' time."

And a third—

"This ain't noathin'; I seed thirteen wherries in this 'ere basin onest."

At last, with much tramping and shoving, we got packed into our places. If you know Loddon basin, you can imagine six wherries manoeuvring there on a pitch black drizzling November night with only a lantern to work by—indeed, our chief amusement at Loddon was to manoeuvre in the rain.

A more romantic and poetic picture was painted by "An Inhabitant" in a little book entitled "Our Town".

And there upon the quay displayed
Black diamonds we see,—
(For much "Our Town" appreciates
That sort of jewelrie)
Whilst on the river—day and night—
Propelled by sail, or quant,
Are wherries bringing for our use
Whatever we may want.

Wherries continued to trade up the Chet until about 1938, but they were mostly small ones, for the water was shallow and the corners awkward. Occasionally large ones did use the river, but usually only half laden.

The North River may appear to the summer holidaymaker to be a very natural sort of waterway, but the hand of man is to be seen in several places in its present course and the Bure is today a very different river from that known to the keelmen of the early eighteenth century. The river between the present mouth of the Ant and the dyke leading to South Walsham Broad is an artificial cut, probably made under an eighteenth-century Act of Parliament for improving the navigation of the Bure. It cut off a sizeable loop of the river and provided a short cut for the trading wherries. Higher up they took another short cut through Hoveton Great Broad, entering either by Polled Ash Dyke or Gravel Dyke, according to the direction of the wind, and gaining access to the river again lower down at The Dam, near Woodbastwick Old Hall.

There was a move in 1869 to make the Muckfleet navigable for wherries so that these craft could penetrate to the Ormesby-Rollesby-Filby group of broads, a proposition that had been discussed for many years. The Muckfleet never was made navigable, but other such dykes were accessible to wherry traffic.

Tunstall Dyke, for instance, leading from the Bure near Stokesby, carried wherry traffic up to Tunstall Staithe, a rather desolate spot in the marshes some distance from the village of Tunstall. To get up to the staithe wherries had to negotiate two awkward bridges, a hump-backed bridge carrying the Acle New Road and a girder bridge carrying the Acle-Yarmouth railway line. It was too narrow for a wherry to tack, and when the wind was contrary the wherry had to be bow-hauled by helpers from Tunstall.

The last wherry to trade up to Tunstall Staithe was the *Albert and Alexandra,* owned by Joseph Powley, who had a wooden house at Tunstall and appeared in Kelly's directory as coal merchant and wherry owner. She continued to use the dyke until about 1897, by which time the dyke was badly silted up and trading had become more than a little difficult. If the water was too high the wherry could not get under the bridges, if it was too low there was not sufficient depth to float the craft; sometimes when the *Albert and Alexandra* was light the plug would be taken out and water allowed to flow into the hold to reduce the wherry's height by an inch or two, which was usually enough to let her get under the bridges.

A wherry in Geldeston lock on its way up to Bungay. The mast has probably been hoisted at the photographer's request; normally it would remain lowered while in the lock.

Quanting a wherry into a lock. The bars across each end of the lock ensured that a wherry was not sailed into the lock, with consequent risk of ramming the far gates and putting them out of operation.

Today Aylsham is well outside the Norfolk Broadland. But there was a time when wherries sailed up the Bure through locks at Coltishall, Buxton Lamas, Oxnead, Burgh and Aylsham to the staithe and mill pool at Aylsham. In the early eighteenth century corn for the weekly market at Aylsham was unloaded from sea-going vessels at Cromer or from wherries at Coltishall and brought by waggon to the town, but in 1773 an Act of Parliament was obtained "for making and extending the navigation of the river Bure, commonly called the North river, by and from Coltishall to Aylsham bridge."

Cargoes expected to be carried on the river above Coltishall can be judged from the list of tolls listed in the Act: 1s. for every ton of coal, bricks, etc; 1s. 6d. for every ton of grain, timber or goods, etc. Two-thirds only was to be paid on cargoes carried from or to Skeyton Beck which passed through only the two lower locks. Muck, marl, etc. for the improvement of land lying near the canal was to be exempt from toll, as was material for the repair of the mills.

A survey was carried out before application was made to Parliament, and the cost was estimated at £4,006 5s. 4½d., a nice if inaccurate piece of tendering. The work began on June 29th, 1774, but by October, 1777, it was little more than half way to completion and already £3,600 had been spent. A Mr. John Smith caused consternation by estimating that another £2,951 would be needed to complete the job. On February 25th, 1778, Mr. Smith agreed to complete the work for the amount mentioned in his estimate, and in March the following year he was joined by Mr. John Green, of Wroxham.

Considerable difficulty had been experienced in obtaining credit for the additional money required, but the commissioners appointed to control the canal came to the rescue and the work was finally completed in October, 1779. Vessels of 13 tons burthen carrying nine chaldrons of coal and drawing not more than 2 feet 4 inches could then reach Aylsham.

For most of its length between Coltishall and Aylsham the course of the river remained for the most part unaltered, but in the parish of Aylsham a new canal leaving the river about a mile below the mill was cut running close to the left bank of the river up to the basin by the staithe. From this a small cut entered the mill pool so that wherries could load corn or flour direct from the mill.

For more than a century the navigation played an important part in the mercantile life of the town, a brisk trade being carried on in corn, coal, timber and other cargoes. At one time as many as 26 wherries were trading to Aylsham, a number being owned in the town.

Aylsham's water-borne trade declined after the railway came to the town, but it was the 1912 flood which finally killed it. Damage, chiefly to the locks, would have cost an estimated £4,000 to repair. The Commissioners of the Navigation Company, with their diminished income, had no resources from which to meet this expenditure, an appeal to the Government was fruitless and the navigation had to be abandoned.

The wherry *Zulu*, owned by Cook, of Aylsham Mill, was imprisoned at Aylsham when Buxton lock was damaged by the flood. She was hauled out at Buxton and launched on the downstream side of the damaged lock by workmen from Allen's yard at Coltishall, being hauled out in the same manner in which it would have been done in a boat-builder's yard, with a winch, planks and all the usual gear. Buxton lock was filled in during 1933.

North Walsham was another town which once was linked to the other East Norfolk waterways by a canal. The North Walsham and Dilham Canal ran from just above Wayford Bridge on the Ant to Antingham Ponds, a distance of rather more than eight miles. There were four locks, only the first of which, at Honing, boasted of a lock-keeper. From him wherrymen collected the key which operated the other three, at Briggate, East Bridge and Bacton Wood.

A Bungay wherry leaving Ellingham lock.

At a meeting at the King's Arms Inn at North Walsham in 1811 it was decided to petition Parliament for a Bill for making a canal from Wayford Bridge to Lingate Common, North Walsham, and there is, at the office of the Clerk of the Peace for Norfolk, a "Plan of the navigable canal proposed to be made from Wayford Bridge to Lingate Common in the County of Norfolk" drawn up by J. Millington, of Hammersmith, in 1815. The canal kept to the east side of the river Ant except for the section from its beginning as far as East Ruston, where a cut went off to the north following the course of the old river. Here a corner was cut off on the west.

A drop in water level of 48 feet is shown from the "head reservoir" above Swafield Mill to Wayford Bridge; there were to be four locks, at Swafield Mill, Bacton Wood Mill, Walsham Mill and Briggate Mill. Dilham Mill was to be passed without a lock.

A second plan deposited at the same office shows a canal sticking to the west side of the river throughout its length and finishing in a basin at Brackenbury Falgate. This would have necessitated another lock, it seems, as the course would have brought the canal over the 50 feet contour.

But it was not until 1824 that it was agreed to go ahead with the building of the canal. Work began under the direction of Mr. Millington on April 5th of the following year, about 60 of the workmen assembling in North Walsham market place and marching

28

with a band to Austin Bridge, where the first flag of turf was cut by Mr. William Youard, the clerk of the sub-committee. The men worked for only a few minutes that day before returning to the market place to partake of some barrels of beer.

Some of the goods conveyed to and from North Walsham and surrounding villages had hitherto been carried to or from a private staithe in Dilham belonging to a Mr. Israel Lewis. As the goods were carried in his wherries he obtained considerable profit as a carrier, and it appeared "on very moderate computation" that he got £200 a year from his possession of the staithe. At the county sessions in 1825 a jury assessed at £1,500 the damages to which Mr. Lewis was entitled owing to the building of the canal.

Thousands of people gathered to watch the first laden wherries sail up the canal to Mr. Cubitt's mill at North Walsham in June, 1826, and according to a newspaper account, "the day finished with a plentiful treat to the workmen of Mr. Sharpe's strong ale and Barclay's brown stout." The canal was formally opened on August 29th that year.

It had cost £32,000 raised in shares of £50 each, but it was confined to small wherries of 10 or 12 tons and drawing not more than 3 feet 6 inches. Because of the dimensions of the locks wherries using the canal were limited to a length of 50 feet and a beam of 12 feet 4 inches.

The tonnage rates were frequently altered, but in 1844 3d. per ton per mile was levied on corn and flour, 1½d. on manure and marl, 3d. on coal and 1½d. on goods. The average receipts each year, between the opening of the canal and 1844, seem to have been about £360. Because of the expensive dues coal was usually brought to North Walsham overland after being landed at Mundesley or Bacton by coasting vessels which unloaded on the beach.

A wherry at Ebridge Mills, on the North Walsham and Dilham Canal.

The canal was deepened at Dilham and Ruston in 1874 by emptying the locked part of the canal, damming it top and bottom in 300-yard sections and barrowing out the gravel bed of the canal with a large labour force from nearby farms.

By a private Act of Parliament passed in 1866 the canal company was authorised to sell the undertaking and to divide the purchase money among the proprietors of the shares. The canal was sold to Edward Press, the North Walsham miller, in 1866 for £600, and the capital dividend of 28s. per share on the 446 shares whose owners were known was declared. The principal clerk had paid out only 55 shares when the remaining money disappeared.

The canal again changed hands in 1907, being sold to a London firm for £2,250.

The North Walsham Canal did not escape damage in the freshwater floods of 1912 which created such havoc in East Norfolk. The west bank of the canal broke just above Bacton Wood lock, and at Ebridge road material was scoured into the canal.

Further changes of ownership took place in 1921, the canal being bought by E. G. Cubitt and G. Walker for £1,500 and then transferred to the North Walsham Canal Co. Ltd. for the same price. Three years later the canal was dredged from Wayford Bridge to Bacton Wood lock by a small pontoon dredger, but in March, 1927, the upper reaches from Swafield lock to Antingham were decanalised—in fact navigation above Swafield Bridge had ceased during the 1890s.

Navigation on the canal as a whole ceased in 1935, and eventually the canal silted up until there was but a trickle of water between the reeds and dredging had to be carried out to maintain effective land drainage.

Suggestions have been made that some of these old navigations should be reopened to provide additional cruising water for holiday traffic, but it seems unlikely that the money necessary for rebuilding locks and dredging silted channels will be forthcoming in the foreseeable future. More likely Bungay, Aylsham and North Walsham will be left to dream of their maritime past while the reeds grow by the forgotten staithes and the drainage water trickles past in channels which would not now bear a dinghy, let alone a wherry.

Acle Bridge about 1900, with a pleasure wherry negotiating the central arch.

CHAPTER TWO

Construction of the Wherry

T HE WHERRY was no bluff, unhandy barge. In general they were graceful and often beautiful vessels admirably suited for navigating the Norfolk and Suffolk waterways on which they developed.

The lines of a wherry of the late nineteenth century, when this craft had reached the peak of development, just as the evolution of sea-going sailing vessels was reaching its climax in the lovely clippers, were fine on the waterline and well rounded on deck. Generally they had a stern curving in to the sternpost in much the same way as the bow curved into the stem, but a few had a transom. In the later days only a handful were transom sterned; in 1948 a 70-year-old wherryman, still at work, could remember five, *Maria,* from the North River, *George,* owned in King Street, Norwich, *Heron,* a pleasure wherry, *Rachel,* and *Elizabeth,* which was then still afloat as a houseboat. But in the first half of the nineteenth century it seems probable that many wherries had this affinity with the old keels. Prints and paintings suggest that quite a high proportion of the craft then sailing the Yare were flat-sterned; the transom was almost always painted white.

The white quadrant painted on the bows was there, so wherrymen said, to make the wherry visible at night to others sailing the same waterway. Some have sought to find the origin of the "white snout" in the oculus of ancient times, but unhappily for their theories there is no continuity of use; judging from illustrations in which wherries figure the white patch on the bows is a mid-nineteenth century introduction which never became universal.

The wherries were always clinker-built of oak, that is with overlapping strakes of two-inch oak, usually fourteen on each side of the keel. A large wherry of over 40 tons had sixteen. Among the traders there was only one exception, that being the *Albion,* built at Oulton Broad in 1898 and now owned by the Norfolk Wherry Trust. Two or three small pleasure wherries built by Collins at Wroxham, including the *Liberty,* were also carvel built, but most pleasure wherries followed the normal pattern. Even the ungainly *Ardea,* built of teak by Leo Robinson at Oulton Broad in 1927, was of clinker construction.

The keel, stem and sternpost were all of oak. The frames, also of oak, were chosen because they had grown to shape and fitted in such a way as to give elasticity to the whole vessel.

There were only two main transverse beams, one at the forward end of the hold and the other at the after end. These were strongly supported by massive hanging and lodging knees. A few wherries had a third beam across the hold amidships.

A transom-sterned wherry lying at Barton Turf. The winch is of the old pattern supported by iron brackets on the tabernacle cheeks.

Supported by the shelf, a fore-and-aft timber fixed to the upper ends of the frames, and by uprights resting on the frames near the turn of the bilge and fastened to the hatch coamings were the side decks, known to wherrymen as the plankways, made usually of single broad planks. What is known in other craft as the covering board, the plank which covers the tops of the frames, is called by the wherryman the planksheer, an old boatbuilding term which has now largely disappeared. It was always painted white so that the deck edge should be visible to the wherryman when he was quanting home on dark, windless nights, as he not infrequently had to do before the advent of auxiliary motors.

The edge of the deck was known as the binns and was surrounded by the binn iron, which protected the wooden deck from scraping and similar damage. The same iron, which was rounded in section, was known as the harpen iron where it passed round the projection of the stem. Wherrymen spoke of a wherry being loaded down to the binns, which meant that "a robin could drink off the deck," as they used to put it.

Loaded to the binns at Yarmouth, in salt water, a wherry had water over the plankways when it reached the fresh water of Norwich.

The hatch coamings, or standing right-ups as they were termed by wherrymen, stood about a foot high and were fitted to the upright struts already mentioned resting on the frames near the turn of the bilge. On top of these were fitted the shifting right-ups, which could be removed for ease of unloading; they slotted into the right-up stanchions, which could also be removed when required. The stanchion on either side of the hold nearest the bow was generally fixed, as was the foremost section of shifting right-up, but the others fitted into chamfered pieces of timber bolted to the inside of the standing right-ups.

The shifting right-ups, which were almost invariably painted white, were slotted on the upper edge to receive the purlins of the hatch covers. These were made in fifteen or sixteen two-foot sections which fitted across the full width of the hold and were cambered so they should shed water easily. They were made in such a way that they provided a watertight covering to the hold, although it was usual to cover them with a tarpaulin for extra security when carrying any cargo which would be damaged by wet. Each section had a small Roman numeral carved on its end, for each would fit only in its proper place.

The fore beam and tabernacle of the *Secunda*. Part of the ceiling on the starboard side has been removed, revealing the heavy timbers.

As the hatch covers were designed to hold one another down and provide a waterproof covering it was necessary to provide certain covers which were not inter- locking, known for obvious reasons as the taking-up hatches. These were usually the third or fourth from each end and the centre one between those two; thus in a wherry with fifteen hatches the taking-up hatches were generally Nos. IV, VIII and XII. The *Eudora,* which had sixteen hatch covers, had Nos. IV, VIII and XIII as the taking-up hatches. Those wherries which were arranged so that the hatches could be locked down for security reasons, as mentioned in the chapter on "unlawful occasions," had only one taking-up hatch.

Some wherries, among them the *Norfolk Hero,* the *Tiger,* the *William* and the *Lucy,* did not follow the more usual practice and had a fore-and-aft beam running down the centre line of the hold. They were fitted with half-hatches, which could be more easily handled by one man, who could twist them over one by one and pile them up sufficiently to facilitate the loading and unloading of cargo. In wet weather these half-hatches had advantages, as only a small part of the hold need be uncovered at a time.

The tabernacle in which the mast swung was fitted at the forward end of the hold, the two stout pieces of oak forming the cheeks being supported by two massive knees resting on the main beam. The mast swung on a pintle in an open iron-shod bearing in the top of the cheeks.

In order to balance the hefty 40-foot mast, which consisted of a single spar, the foot carried a great block of lead or iron, the former being the more usual as the yards on which the wherries were built could cast a lead weight on the spot. Cast iron weights had to be made at a foundry and then transported to the boatyard to be fitted. Various weights have been given for these balances; a researcher once calculated the weight of the balance fitted to the mast of the *Gleaner* as 1 ton 12 cwt.

In earlier days English larch was used for the masts, but a certain Martin Barber, master of the *Maid of Yare,* a brig trading from Yarmouth to the Baltic ports noticed that the larch masts, many of which came from Costessey Park, were constantly breaking under the strain of the large sail. On his next trip to the Baltic he brought back four pitchpine trees, which were made into masts and fitted into Pope's wherries of St. Margaret's Wharf, Norwich. Those early pitchpine masts were as red as cherries, according to William Royall, the wherryman who told this story. These first pitchpine masts were fitted to the *Eclipse, Progress, Prospect* and *Thomas Maria.* The masts of the first three did eventually break, but their lives were very much longer than those of the larch masts; the spar put into the *Thomas Maria* never did break, and was eventually used for some other purpose.

Old masts could often be cut down and used for some purpose or other, but few can have been cut into planks and used to build a traditional broads type of double-ended fishing punt as one was in 1940 when wood was hard to find.

Hoisting sail (left). The luff is taut and the peak is rising; the gaff line has not yet been taken forward. Lowering sail (right). The helmsman holds the peak inboard with the gaff line as the mate eases away on the winch.

When the mast was lowered the foot, with the great balance weight bolted to it, rose up through the carling hatch, a narrow opening in the foredeck normally covered with the carling board, a small forepeak hatch. This hatch also gave admittance to the fore-peak, which for the purpose of working out the registered tonnage was referred to as the sail room. It was generally used as a store and as a convenient place from which to pump out the bilges with the old wooden swipe which all wherries used to carry. On occasion the mate would even sleep down there if the cabin was otherwise in use, the rough rack on which gear was stacked being used as a bunk when necessary.

Just ahead of the mast was the winch, used to hoist the sail. This was usually fitted to two timber stanchions bedded on to the frames and rising through the foredeck, al-though on some wherries it was fitted to iron brackets which were bolted to the taber-nacle cheeks. It seems likely that this was a survival of the earliest form of winch fitted to wherries; the small wherries of the latter part of the eighteenth century were not fitted with winches at all. The barrel of the winch was made to swing aside when it was re-quired to lower the mast in order to let the foot of that spar swing upwards.

The wherryman's home was the little cabin in the stern, the roof of which followed the same line as the hatches. One of the furnishings of the cabin was a stove, the chimney of which was carried through the cabin roof at the forward end. To prevent the sheet blocks or the foot of the sail from fouling this chimney it was faired by a wooden construction known as the coburg. Above this fitted a wooden chimney, which might be either fairly short or fairly tall according to the wherryman's fancy; it was of course shipped only when the wherry was moored and was removed when the sail was set.

The coburg was sometimes made to slide into position between two pieces of wood fixed to the cabin top and over a piece of wood in the centre which was also made fast to the cabin top. The purpose of this was so that the coburg could be removed when it was necessary to pile the hatches on the fore end of the cabin roof.

When under way the wherryman stood at the tiller just outside the door of his cabin. In what were known as low sternsheets wherries the skipper steered from a small well, from which he entered the cabin through two small doors, while in what were termed by the waterside fraternity high sternsheets wherries the helmsman stood on deck and entered his cabin by way of a cabin slip and two or three steps. In the latter type, which was peculiar to the Norwich River, the tiller was curved sharply upwards so that the inboard end was at the level of the helmsman's waist, while in the low sternsheets wherry the tiller was more or less straight. One wherryman of my acquaintance once said that he preferred sailing a low sternsheets wherry, for when sailing one without a well in a really strong wind it was possible to be helped overboard by the tiller. Wherries of the high sternsheets type never had white snouts.

Wherrymen were, of necessity, careful of their rigging, for if the forestay, or spring stay as they called it, were to break the mast would come down and the gaff perhaps break. In 1929 just such an accident occurred to the *Hilda* when close-hauled near Horning Ferry. Mast, gaff and sail came crashing down as the forestay parted, yet practically no damage was done except that the winch and its supports were wrenched away as the foot of the mast swung up. It was, however, an awkward job retrieving the sail and gaff which had fallen into the river.

The forestay was, in fact, the only standing rigging used on wherries. It was of wire, with an eye spliced into the top to fit over the masthead and with a tackle at the foot, this tackle consisting of a double block attached to the stay and a single block at the lower end. This single block was on a long iron bar which was in turn hooked to the stem-head eyebolt; on the iron bar was a cleat to which the end of the tackle was belayed.

The tackle itself was of manila or hemp, the latter being preferred as manila tended to stretch and was more liable to shrinkage in wet conditions. Sometimes when the tackle stretched the masthead would drop as much as a foot; then, when the wherry was in a favourable reach and before the wind, one of the crew would have to go forward to tighten the tackle.

Some wherries had a ring spliced into the bottom of the stay, and after belaying the tackle the running end would be led up through the ring and belayed a second time. This gave greater security should the tackle part, and was particularly used on timber-hauling wherries which used the mast as a derrick for loading heavy logs.

The single halyard, which was rove in such a way that it raised both throat and peak, was of tarred hemp. Passing upwards from the winch and through the "herring hole" over a large sheave set within the broadened section of the masthead, the halyard was then rove through a single block at the throat, then through one sheave of a double block suspended from the "crane iron" at the masthead and taken out to the span block, a single block fitted to the spans (see below), over the other sheave of the double block and down to the gaff, being made fast close to the throat.

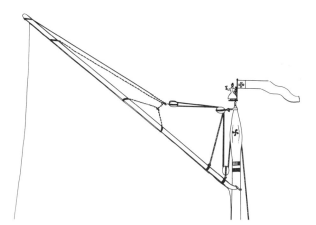

Rigging of gaff on a wherry.

The gaff, which in a big wherry might be as much as 40ft. long, was suspended by a system of "spans" as can be seen in the drawing. Early wherries with much shorter gaffs did not need the complicated arrangement of spans seen in the late nineteenth and twentieth century wherries.

Nor did they have winches for raising the sail, but they did make use of a rather complicated arrangement for raising the peak. Instead of the standing part of the halyard being made fast to the gaff it was brought down the port side of the mast, terminating in a series of single-whip purchases. This continued to be used in a few wherries after the introduction of winches, and can be seen in a model of the *Norfolk Hero* in the Maritime Museum for East Anglia at Yarmouth. One of the last wherries so fitted was Gay's *Emma* from Irstead.

The halyard was not just a piece of rope of uniform size. A typical halyard consisted of 30 fathoms of 3 inch or $3\frac{1}{2}$ inch rope with a tail of about eight fathoms of $1\frac{1}{2}$

inch stuff joined to one end by a long splice. The tail was coiled first on the winch, when the strain on the halyard was least, and run on to half the barrel, so that the halyard should take up as little room as possible on the barrel and so that there should still be a fair purchase when the peak was being set.

Special halyards which tapered throughout their length were made by a Yarmouth ropemaker named Neave, and wherries in the timber trade which used to have to lift logs of as much as four tons with the halyard also had special halyards made for them in Norwich. A new halyard would be needed about three times a year, but if they were made of inferior cordage they did not last as long as four months—and then there was trouble.

When the halyard was used for handling cargo it was taken out of the herring hole and rove through a block which was chained to the mast about the level of the painted bands below the herring hole. A careful wherryman would use a sack to prevent the chain from biting into the mast, which was partly lowered so that it served as a make-shift derrick.

Hoisting sail in a wherry was quite different from the same operation in any other vessel. As the wherryman cranked rapidly away on the winch all the initial lift was on the crutch block, the throat rising until the luff was tight. Once the crutch block could rise no further the hoist was transferred to the span block and the peak began to rise. To prevent the gaff from taking control during this operation the master would have to hang on to the gaff line, a length of rope made fast to the outer end of the gaff, and pay it out gradually as the mate cranked away at the winch. The gaff line was used only when hoisting or lowering sail, and when the wherry was under sail it would be taken forward and the running end placed through the lower reef cringle or through one of the lower mast hoops; it was customary to loop it loosely and not to make it fast, so that if it fouled the branches of a riverside tree it would be shaken loose without causing any damage. When setting the peak, the heaviest part of the job, the mate was able to engage a lower gear by transferring the winch handle to a lower shaft, called the patten bar.

The sail of a wherry had an area of around 1,200 square feet. It was made fast to the gaff by robands, separate pieces of rope passed round the spar and tied, each being fixed to an eyelet in the head of the sail; the luff was seized to mast hoops and the sail was loose-footed, without a boom. An additional section termed the bonnet could be laced to the foot to extend the area of the sail. There were three rows of reef points.

A number of sailmakers specialised in making wherry sails, one of them being Robert Pike, who died in 1940 at the age of 79. His father had started as a sailmaker at a loft on Yarmouth's North Quay in 1883 and he himself carried on there until 1933, when he retired owing to failing sight. Another Yarmouth sailmaker who turned out sails for wherries was Walter Garrod.

When first set a new sail would be as white as any yacht's sail, but once it was decently stretched it would be painted with a mixture of coal tar, never Stockholm tar,

The *Dispatch* stretching a new sail before it is dressed, a photograph taken in September, 1932. The bonnet is laced to the foot of the sail, but so light is the wind that the mate is quanting.

herring oil and lamp-black. Neatsfoot oil used to be preferred to herring oil, possibly because it was so good for waterproofing leather boots; two gallons would be bought for dressing the sail, and that no doubt left some over for the footwear.

The sail would be spread out on top of the hatches, the paintwork being protected with a tarpaulin, and the mixture would be applied on one side with a tar brush. Along the lines of reef points and along the luff, where the sail was of double thickness, it was necessary to paint the canvas on both sides; elsewhere the mixture soaked through, though at the first dressing the sail would have a greyish complexion on one side. About six months after the first dressing the opposite side of the sail would be painted with the black mixture, and thereafter the sail would be dressed on alternate sides at yearly intervals.

Mr. Walter Powley, who sailed in the *Maud* and the *Dora,* has told me that he treated the sail in March, in order that the tar and oil should be dry when the wherry went to Reedham for repainting, which she did every June.

This kind of dressing gave a characteristic black appearance to the sail. Only two wherries are remembered as having brown sails; they were the *Myth* and the *Wanderer,* both Lowestoft craft, which had their sails tanned like the sails of the smacks fishing from that port.

Loaded down to the binns, a wherry goes about; the mate is helping her head round by using the quant.

The bigger wherries carried three sets of sheet blocks, the wherryman choosing the size of his set according to the amount of wind. The smallest set of blocks, the "dandy blocks" as they were called, were fitted with roller bearings, and through these the sheet would run out with much clattering and squeaking. To the biggest set of blocks could be added a single-sheave block termed a becket block in the worst of weather; whether it fitted inside the inner or outer sheet block depended on the arrangement and the number of sheeves in these blocks.

In rough weather when the biggest set of blocks and the becket block were in use it was not unusual to fit a relieving tackle to the tiller, one block being attached to the timberhead and the other to the tiller. When it was blowing really hard the mate would have to lend a hand on the end of the tackle, standing on the plankway with one foot placed in the open cabin scuttle to give him a strong position.

In normal weather the wherryman used to steer not so much with his hands as with his back, which he would use to push the heavy wooden tiller from side to side when tacking. After a fresh blow a wherryman's back would sometimes be chafed almost raw.

Sailing with a crew of two was hard work in a strong breeze, but when the trade declined and cargoes were only obtained at uncertain intervals the wherryman who owned his own craft had to manage as best he could without a mate because of diminishing receipts, and then it was heavy work indeed. Tom Lodge, master of the 40-ton wherry *Macadam,* which used to carry stone and other materials for repairing roads, used to sail single-handed and also load and unload the 40 tons of road material without help. Thanks to years of experience and an uncanny knowledge of what his craft would do he used to manage all right, but in lowering his sail he was at a disadvantage. He could not stand by the winch and at the same time use the gaff line to prevent that spar from swinging over the side as it was lowered. How often he must have wished that the luff of the sail would go down first so that the gaff would hang by the peak, straight up and down the mast; he could then have lashed it to the mast until such time as he could safely moor his craft.

However, he found a way of doing the job unaided. When lowering sail in a small wherry he lowered the gaff until it was more-or-less horizontal, then he ran aft and made the gaff line fast at the sternsheets; returning forward he would lower away again until the end of the gaff touched the top of the cabin, when he would release the pawl on the winch and, with the halyard in one hand, walk across the hatches to seize the gaff with the other hand—he could then let go of the halyard and allow the gaff and sail to rattle down on to the hatches.

In a bigger wherry, with heavier gear, he would first ease off the forestay so that the mast raked aft, then lower the peak until the gaff rested on the cabin top; at a suitable moment when the sail was as near the centre of the hatches as possible he would allow

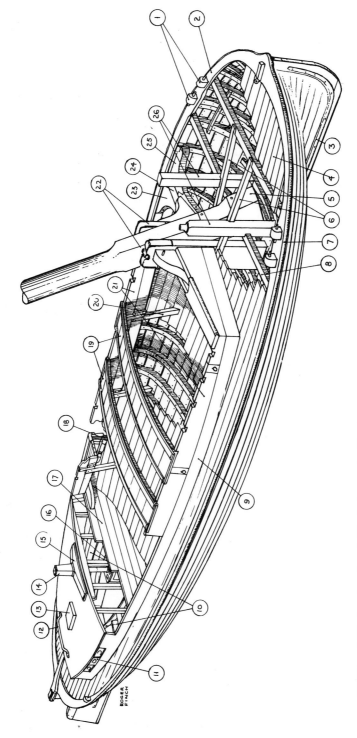

KEY—1) Timber heads. 2) Planksheer. 3) Slipping keel irons. 4) Deck planking. 5) Mast counter weight. 6) Fore hatch coamings. 7) Iron rubbing band. 8) Deck beams. 9) Standing right ups. 10) Cabin bunks. 11) Cabin lights. 12) Main horse. 13) Cabin hatch. 14) Removable chimney. 15) Coburg. 16) Cabin Stove. 17) After bulkhead. 18) Clamp. 19) Hatch covers. 20) Stanchions. 21) Shifting right ups. 22) Tabernacle cheeks. 23) Knees. 24) Mainbeam. 25) Lodging knees. 26) Winch stanchions.

the luff to run down the mast, the force of the gaff and sail coming down jerking the mast upright. It was then a simple job to take up the slack of the forestay. While going through these evolutions the tiller would be held with a line.

In such experienced hands as those of Tom Lodge a wherry could be made to do almost anything demanded of it, but in the hands of a novice she might easily run amok. Many amateurs have after considerable practice learned to sail wherries without mishap, but it needed a lifetime of experience to take advantage of every slight change in wind direction, to make the best of every scant reach and to cover the ground in the shortest possible time.

With an easterly wind a wherry could sail from Yarmouth to Norwich without tacking. The Devil's House Reach below Cantley and Coldham Hall Reach would be very close hauled, but if the wherry was well laden and had plenty of way it could get through without a tack.

Tom Lodge claimed to have sailed a wherry from the railway swing bridge just below Norwich to the Knoll at the entrance of the North River at Yarmouth, the two points between which wherrymen normally timed their passages on the Norwich River, in three hours twenty minutes. Wherrymen reckoned that you could only sail from Norwich to Yarmouth in this time and that it took longer sailing in the opposite direction because the ebb tide is generally much stronger than the flood. With a strong ebb tide a wherry could always sail from Reedham to Yarmouth in an hour, providing the wind was reasonably strong; it was rare to accomplish the return journey on the flood in the same time.

The tide is certainly something to be taken into account. Whether the effect of the tide has really changed a great deal owing to the dredging of Yarmouth harbour, the silting of Breydon and other factors is still somewhat a matter of argument, but certainly wherrymen speak of it as no sluggish, easy current. One has only to watch the tide sluicing out through the Haven Bridge at Yarmouth, and to remember that the wherries dropped down into the harbour to load their cargoes from sea-going ships day by day, to realise that the Norfolk waterman could never afford to forget the tide. Even in the upper reaches of the river the tide, while it has a rise and fall of only a few inches, ebbs and flows enough to make itself felt. Floodwater, rushing down from the hinterland of Norfolk and pouring through the bridges of Norwich, was something to be reckoned with, and reckoned with very seriously, in the days of the wherry trade.

Walter Powley, a member of a family which was well known on the Norfolk water-ways, has told of some of his fast passages between Norwich and Yarmouth, and of some that remained fixed in his memory for just the opposite reason. In the *Maud* he came to Norwich with roadstone, unloaded and returned to Yarmouth the same day. In the latter part of the nineteenth century the "pubs" opened at 6 a.m., and his mate, Victor Welton, was able to get a pint at a Yarmouth public house before they left about 6.30. At Trowse Eye, the junction of the Yare and Wensum, the wherry was discharged by Norwich Corporation workmen and while they got the cargo, almost 40 tons of it, out of the hold Mr. Powley walked away up to the *Heartsease,* a public house on the Plumstead Road, to get the money for it. As soon as he got back they started on the return journey, and despite the fact that the wind failed them at Reedham they arrived at Yarmouth about 10.30 p.m.—and Vic Welton nipped ashore and was able to get another pint at the same pub before closing time at 11 p.m., much to the landlord's surprise.

When the wind was contrary, or more frequently when there was no wind at all, the wherryman had to resort to quanting. The quant was a 22 foot pole, with a turned wood "bott" or knob at its head and a wooden heel to prevent it sinking into the mud and iron toe at its foot. The man walked to the bows of the wherry, pushed the quant into the bed of the river, put the bott to his shoulder and walked along the plankway towards the stern. On reaching the sternsheets he twisted and withdrew the quant from the mud with a deft turn of the wrist and marched back to the bows to resume his labour.

A yachtsman, laboriously quanting his little vessel along on a hot afternoon with much the same technique as the undergraduate propelling his punt past the colleges of Cambridge, cannot appreciate the real art of quanting. Aboard a wherry there were no shrouds to complicate the business, a man had something like forty feet to walk each time he thrust the quant into the riverbed, and he had a really businesslike quant into the bargain—indeed, when the river was deepened by dredging the watermen favoured a 24 foot quant in place of the older 22-footer.

Quanting was very heavy labour if carried on for any great distance and any long period. Walter Powley remembered loading a cargo at Whitbread's maltings in King Street, Norwich, one Saturday. They did not leave until between 5.30 and 5.45 p.m., and the cargo had to be at Yarmouth for unloading on the Monday morning. There was not a breath of wind and Powley and his mate, a man named Brown on this occasion, quanted all the way to Seven Mile House, going below one at a time for food and a cup of tea. A thick fog lay over the river and they ran ashore by Surlingham brickyard, but they managed to shove clear again and to keep going, though many times during that trip he almost fell asleep as he pushed the laden wherry on its way. In the morning the fog cleared and sail was hoisted at Seven Mile House, as there was then just enough wind to take them over Breydon and into Yarmouth, where they arrived at eleven o'clock on the Sunday morning. After all that labour he received about eight or nine shillings for that trip.

When he told that story he said nothing of the tide, but clearly it served him well enough or he would not have quanted and sailed all that 30 miles or so in some $17\frac{1}{2}$ hours. When the tides did not serve there was nothing to do but wait, and on one occasion Powley had to leave his wherry moored by the *Stracey Arms* on the North River and walk home to Yarmouth, covering the seven miles in about two hours.

William Royall never claimed to have covered the 27 miles from Norwich swing bridge to the Knoll at Yarmouth in less than three hours and fifteen or twenty minutes, but he used to say that when the *Spray,* the wherry in which he traded for so many years, was first built she had been sailed to Yarmouth by George Amis in just three hours. The sail was at that time new and undressed, and there was consequently a great saving of weight which may have accelerated the timing.

Stories of fast trips on the other rivers are fewer, but a tale is told of a wherryman who left Geldeston at 6.15 a.m. with some eels and had cooked them and eaten them before 10 p.m. the same day at Wroxham.

On the North River C. Rump, who sailed the *Hilda* until she sank at Horning in 1940, told of sailing from Yarmouth to Coltishall in five hours, though he reckoned in 1930 that at that time he was lucky to get from Yarmouth to Wroxham in six or six and a half hours. "We don't get the winds we use to," he explained, blaming that new-fangled invention of Marconi for taking the weight out of the wind. In fact it seems far more likely that the growth of trees along the river banks was responsible.

One of the most-publicised capabilities of the wherry was an ability to sail remarkably close to the wind. In fact it is unlikely that in open water a wherry could point any higher than any other fore-and-aft rigged vessel, but both rig and hull were ideally suited to local conditions, and the hollow bow built up a "wedge" of water between the vessel and the river bank which held the wherry off a lee shore. Instead of hugging the weather bank as most vessels do the wherry would creep along the lee shore, the bow being pushed off from time to time as necessary by the mate with a quant.

Although designed for work in shallow waters where anything which increased the draught was frowned on, the wherry had a rockered external keel which undoubtedly did much to give her good sailing qualities. On the wherries trading up to Bungay, North Walsham and Aylsham and into other particularly shallow places this was made removable so that the draught could be reduced to the minimum.

The wooden slipping keel was weighted with iron so that it just floated and at the forward end were two irons which fitted on either side of the stem; aft two ropes were passed through holes in the keel, and these had knots in them at an equal distance from the keel. When shipping the keel it was pushed down with a boathook and hauled under the wherry using the ropes fitted near the after end, the iron straps positioning it neatly at the bow. There were three keel bolts passing down into the slipping keel from inside the wherry; when it was slipped the holes were filled by plugs. As soon as the keel was roughly in place a "feeler," a short iron rod of smaller diameter than the pin, was inserted into each hole in turn, the bolt being inserted as soon as the keel was accurately positioned.

The operation of replacing a keel would not take more than a quarter of an hour and only about a bucketful of water would have to be pumped out when the operation was completed. If a wherry had gone aground and had been strained, however, it might take quite a lot longer to get the keel in place.

After being slipped at Geldeston or Coltishall the slipping keel would be left moored to the bank until the wherry returned downstream. It was considered in-advisable to haul them out on to the rond for two reasons; for one thing there was a risk of the keel becoming warped or strained if laid on an uneven surface and for another if it dried out it would be more inclined to float and would be less easy to fit when the time came. In any case it would be too heavy to haul out without great effort.

The honour of having invented the slipping keel has been variously claimed by Jimmy Lacey, who was certainly the first to adopt it up the Bungay River, and by Robert Bates, who died in 1928, and his father at Coltishall. Bob Bates, a white-whiskered old fellow who for long had charge of the pleasure wherry *Gladys,* seems to have the best claim.

The advantages of having a pole mast swinging in a tabernacle, with no standing rigging except the spring stay, were well shown when a wherry came up to a bridge. The wherry would sail almost up to the bridge, and when a collision with the arch seemed almost inevitable the sail would come down, the parrel line on the gaff jaws would be hurriedly cast off and the mast would swing down, the winch having been swung aside to allow the heel to rise. The wherry would normally carry enough way to bring it through the bridge, although the wherryman would need to steer to a nicety while his mate attended to mast and sail, for most of the old bridges were neither too wide nor too high. Immediately the wherry had cleared the arch, up would swing the mast as the mate tallied on the spring stay tackle, then when he had slipped the parrel pin into place on the gaff jaws and swung the winch barrel back into position and dropped the latch to hold it in place he would fit the winch handle and begin to crank away; the throat of the great sail would begin to climb up the mast, and before the vessel had lost way the peak would rise and the wherry would be on its way without a pause.

The watermen, of course, knew the peculiarities of each bridge and how to deal with them. When going under St. Olaves bridge, for instance, one had to be quick to raise the sail if a southerly or south-westerly wind was blowing because of a head wind in the following reach. A loaded wherry had enough weight to carry her on, but a light wherry might get into difficulties.

The narrow-arched brick bridges such as those at Wroxham, Ludham and Potter Heigham were difficult to navigate and were impediments to the larger craft. The bridge at Ludham, which had a groove cut in the brickwork of the arch by the mastheads of wherries passing through, was replaced by an iron girder bridge in the second decade of this century, and after the second world war there was a move to replace Potter Heigham bridge because it was said that it prevented many holiday craft from reaching Hickling and Horsey, and because it was said to be as much a hindrance to road traffic

No room to spare: the pleasure wherry *Cyclops* passing through old Ludham bridge.

as it was to navigation on the Thurne. Road traffic now has a fine new bridge on the line of the old Midland and Great Northern Railway a short distance upstream, but the old bridge remains.

This old bridge, from the lowness of its central arch as much as from its narrowness, was a particularly awkward obstruction to wherry traffic. It is said that one one occasion when floods had raised the water level the master of a wherry bound down from the upper reaches piled heavy stones on deck to ballast his craft down, yet it was only with great difficulty and with the assistance of some old jacks borrowed from a boatyard that she was forced through the bridge.

The old Ludham bridge was a serious obstacle on the River Ant, and at times trading wherries had to wait until slack water before they could get through. Wherries converted for pleasure and with their hatches raised to give headroom to the cabin found particular difficulty here, and the *Elsie* once got jammed in the arch so that it was impossible either to go forward or to force her astern to clear the bridge. Boats on the river both above and below were held up and road traffic over the bridge was stopped as people watched to see how the owner was going to extricate his wherry. Eventually

Another picture of the *Eudora* in dock, with the iron bow straps of the slipping keel visible on the right.

The *Eudora* in Fellows' dock at Yarmouth in 1938. The slipping keelcan be seen lying on the floor of the dock on the left of the picture, with two bolts

no fewer than 110 people were packed on board the wherry, and with this additional weight she just slipped clear.

Another pleasure party stranded above one of these bridges borrowed sacks of flour from a trading wherry lying nearby in order to ballast their wherry so that she could be taken through.

The old bridge at Beccles not only prevented sea-going vessels from proceeding further up the Waveney after the opening of the navigation by way of Lowestoft but proved an obstacle to wherries and in flood time penned up the water to a considerable extent. In severe winters drifting ice was caught by the piles of the bridge and built up against them, forming a barrier both to navigation and to the flow of the river; men had to be stationed along the bridge parapet with weights dangling on ropes to break up the ice.

Wherries might be trapped for days on end above the bridge when the river was running high, for the headroom was very limited. Floodwater held up by the bridge would spread far across the marshes on the Norfolk side of the river and travellers would have to be ferried by boat across Gillingham Dam, and this gave some wherry-men a way round the obstruction. Masters of small wherries returning downstream without cargo would sail across the flooded marshes, regaining the river below Beccles.

If the old-time wherrymen knew how to beat the tide, they also knew how to make it serve them. When dropping down on the tide through the Yarmouth bridges, there were the railway, Suspension and Vauxhall bridges on the North River as well as the Haven Bridge, they lowered their masts and sails and heaved a length of chain, which they kept in the forepeak for this purpose, over the bow. The dropping chain, as it was known, dragged through the mud and held the wherry back, thus enabling the master to steer her down through the bridges stern first.

It was an interesting sight to watch a wherry dropping down through the bridges, often if loaded with a chain out over each bow, moving slowly at first and then faster and faster as it swept nearer and nearer the bridge, the master casting anxious glances astern as he deftly lined up his craft with the opening. As the wherry passed through its speed increased still more, the dropping chain sliding over the stones which had been thrown beneath the bridge to reduce the scour.

Seagoing vessels which had been upriver to Norwich or Beccles used to drag down behind their anchors in the same way—steam tugs were never employed more than was absolutely necessary, and many skippers of the old school long retained a memory of the way things were done before steam was introduced.

The dropping chains, which used to be shackled round one of the winch stanchions or round a timberhead, became highly polished with continued use.

The wherry was at one time as colourful as any part of the Norfolk landscape, if it was not as famous for its decoration as the canal boat of the Midland canals with its castles and roses. The hull was tarred, and G. C. Davies once wrote "we have seen a picture worth painting when a wherry has been canted over by means of a rope from her mast, and in a boat alongside men in the picturesque waterside costume are burning the tar off her bottom with huge torches made of bundles of reeds as big as wheat-sheaves." Alas, this is a picture which will never now be painted, unless it be from the imagination of some modern artist.

The deck was likewise tarred, sawdust or husks being trodden into the molten pitch to give a foothold to the wherryman when quanting. Sometimes wherries had a red segment on the deck at the bow, corresponding with the white snout, as the wherrymen described it, on the sides of the bow to enable the wherry to be seen at night. In contrast to the black deck the planksheer was painted white, so that the deck-edge was visible in darkness.

In all this the wherryman had little chance for decoration, but in painting the rest of his vessel he used bright colours, red, green, blue and yellow. The standing right-ups might be black, blue, or sometimes green, while the shifting right-ups were almost always white. The back of his cabin with the cabin doors gave the wherryman scope for bright panelling and lining in any colours he might choose.

The cabin roof and the hatches were frequently deep red, while some wherries had cream hatches outlined in blue, those of the iron wherry *Vega,* built by Fellows' of Yarmouth for Woods, Sadd, Moore & Co. being coloured thus. The tabernacle was mostly red, while the winch stanchions were usually white.

Flanking the tabernacle were name boards bearing the names of the wherry and its owner and the place from which they hailed, often painted in blue and yellow and sometimes, as in the case of the *Malve,* built as the *Olga* for Isaac Wales, with incised lettering. Some proud owners went to the expense of gold leaf for the name boards.

The squared section at the foot of the mast was painted white and the main section of this stout spar was scraped and varnished or oiled, but the upper part was distinctively painted, with bands and various devices such as circles, stars or the "bunch of pears" around the herring hole. The mast of the *Dispatch,* for instance, had a green top, with a white circle about the herring hole and red, white and blue bands beneath. One of the older generation of Broads yachtsmen once told me that wherrymen he knew used to beg odd pots of paint from him after he had painted his boat so they could colour the mastheads of their wherries. Any bright colour was welcomed, for generally the owner-masters were not consistent in their choice, but some firms owning fleets looked upon the masthead colours as a means of recognition and used the same colour scheme on all their wherries.

Wherrymen could identify wherries from a great distance by the way the top of the sail set. When the wherry got closer and the type of vane and the colour of the

The *Hilda's* masthead and vane.

A moored wherry. The winch is fitted to the tabernacle on iron brackets instead of being mounted on wooden stanchions.

masthead were to be seen their identification would be established without the slightest hesitation, and it was doubtless to the advantage of a big firm to make its wherries clearly distinguishable in this way.

The General Steam Navigation Co. Ltd. had red mastheads with yellow and black bands, while Bessey & Palmer, the Yarmouth coal merchants, had blue mastheads with white and red bands below. Blue mastheads were also adopted by J. & J. Colman, of Carrow Works, Norwich, well known as the firm that made a fortune out of the mustard people left on their plates; in this case the bands were gold and blue. Press Bros. also favoured blue, with yellow and red bands and the addition of a yellow ring around the herring hole, while Woods, Sadd, Moore & Co. topped their royal blue mastheads with a red tip above the crane iron as well as having red, white, red, white bands below. Cubitt & Walker stuck to green mastheads with a yellow band, while W. D. & A. E. Walker adopted bright green with yellow and blue bands and identified individual wherries by giving the *Albion* and the *Hope* a bunch of pears about the herring hole and the *Mayflower* a star. The Surlingham brickworks chose a more subdued scheme of slate grey with two white bands for their two wherries, the *Meteor* and the *Herald*.

The gaff, with a view to economy of upkeep, was invariably painted instead of being varnished, the colour usually chosen being white, with slate grey or red as alternatives. Wherrymen who took real pride in the appearance of their wherries used to unlash the sail from this spar periodically and wash it with soap and water.

All this naturally resulted in a vessel which gave plenty of colour to any scene of which it was a feature, as W. A. Dutt remarked in his book *The Norfolk Broads,* the first edition of which came out in the early 1900s. Speaking of Acle, he wrote: "I remember an evening when two of them were moored near the bridge. They were remarkable for their brilliant hues. The top of the mast and the sides of the hold of one were painted Pyrenese green; the square wooden chimney of the cabin was bright red, as were the rigging blocks and tabernacle; the cabin door was dark blue relieved by yellow bands; and the top of the tiller and its handle, the gaff and flag-frame, were white. The other wherry, which had only that morning left a Coltishall wherry-builder's yard, where it had been repainted, had red, white and blue bands round the top of the mast, and beneath them was a two-feet band of burnished brass; flag, tabernacle blocks and cabin roof were vermilion, and the tiller and cabin door were royal blue and yellow. Both wherries were 'light', and one showed something of a white, the other of a pale green keel. All these colours were reflected in the water, where they shimmered and melted one into another whenever a breath of wind or a passing boat sent ripples running towards the shore."

Some owners took enormous pride in the upkeep of their craft. Jimmy Gibbs, of Surlingham and later of Oulton Broad, was once asked why he took so much trouble over the painting of a trading wherry, and his reply was: "As long as she goes off the Broad looking as smart as the smartest yachts afloat I'll be satisfied."

Perhaps one of the most noticeable ornamentations of the wherry was the vane, which served the purpose of showing the wherryman which way the wind was blowing, no matter how light the wind might be, for the yard of red bunting caught the lightest of airs.

The vane consisted of two horizontal metal rods, the upper one about two feet long and the lower one some six inches shorter, fitted at one end to a vertical iron tube which fitted over an iron rod on the top of the mast. This rod formed the pivot of the vane, which was held on by a brass doorknob screwed on to the top of the rod or on some wherries by a pointed wooden cap. Next the pivot was a device of sheet iron known as the gate. In its simplest form this took the pattern of a six-pointed star, but usually it was more complicated and more decorative. A common device was the "circular saw" or serrated-edged circle containing some emblem, often illustrating the name of the wherry, cut out or painted on. It has been said that the "circular saw" vanes originated on wherries belonging to some timber merchant or other.

Vanes with human figures on the opposite side to the gate acting as balances were very popular. These were generally known as Jenny Morgans, after the hero of a popular song of that name, so it is said. They were also known as Welsh girls, presumably after the same person, and some did depict a lady in a flowerpot hat holding a bunch of leeks.

According to R. H. Teasdel, of Yarmouth, this style of vane was first made for the wherry *Jenny Morgan,* built by Petch Brothers of Norwich about 1856 "on spec," and named after the heroine of a then-popular but now forgotten song. This wherry was used by Rudd in connection with his brick kiln at Rockland, and later by one Bacon for the shipment of deals. Often, however, the figure was not that of a Welsh girl at all, for female figures of various kinds and even male figures made their appearance in later years. A mermaid, a sailor and a trumpeter all graced the mastheads of wherries about the turn of the century.

Mr. Teasdel should know as much as anyone about the origin of these vanes, for his grandfather was a Yarmouth shipchandler who supplied rope, spars, paint and other necessary items to wherries as well as vanes. Other makers of vanes in the same town were a tinsmith named Hatch and Fred Harrod, of Mariners Road, who was recognised as a master at the job.

The *Albion*, built in 1898 for Bungay maltsters W. D. & A. E. Walker, seen at Bungay Staithe.

CHAPTER THREE

Men and Merchandise

THE ORIGIN of the Norfolk wherry is to a great extent lost in the mists of antiquity. Nobody knows for sure quite when this type of vessel first came into use for carrying goods on the East Anglian rivers. One thing is certain: it is a strictly local type and bears no real resemblance to vessels used for carrying cargo on other waters.

Neither the wherry nor its predecessor the keel should be confused with craft bearing similar names in use in other areas, for though the name was the same both hull design and rig were different. Just as the word "punt" was used in different areas for differing types of fishing craft ranging from the double-ended boat of the Norfolk coast and the transom-sterned boat of the Suffolk beaches to the box-like punt of the upper Thames, the words "keel" and "wherry" were used for a wide variety of dissimilar craft.

The *Oxford Dictionary of English Etymology* defines keel as a flat-bottomed vessel or lighter and says that the word, first recorded in the fourteenth century, is derived from the Old English word "coel", being comparable to Dutch and German words with similar pronunciation. The Norfolk keel was not, in fact, flat-bottomed and in hull form was in distinct contrast to the keel of the Yorkshire waterways.

The same dictionary records that the word "wherry" is first used in the sense of a light rowing boat, as found in varying forms on the Thames and at Portsmouth until quite recent times, during the fifteenth century and first used in the sense of a barge in the sixteenth. Refusing to hazard any guess, the compilers admit that the word is "of unknown origin".

Some writers have found a resemblance between the Norfolk wherry and the craft of the Dutch waterways, and some have suggested that it is directly descended from the longships of the Norsemen. But neither would seem to be true if the facts are weighed up carefully.

The basic differences between the keel and the wherry were in rig, although the keel seems to have had a heavier, bluffer and less handy hull. Whereas the keel had its mast amidships and a square sail, the wherry had its mast set in the bows and a loose-footed gaff sail. The Norfolk keel never set a topsail like its namesake on the Yorkshire rivers.

The two types of vessel, keel and wherry, seem to have existed together for at least 200 years, but during that time the obvious advantages of the gaff sail as opposed to the square sail set on a yard drove the keel slowly but surely off the rivers as the wherry increased in numbers. Yet by the time the last keel had passed from the East Anglian scene the heyday of the wherry itself was nearing its end.

By the beginning of the nineteenth century the wherry seems to have been the most numerous type of craft on the rivers, for comparatively few keels appear in pictures of the East Norfolk landscape dating from this period. Indeed, only two keels but a very much larger number of wherries appear in Stark's *River Scenery of Norfolk and Suffolk*, published to commemorate the opening of the Norwich and Lowestoft Navigation.

Early maps and prospects of Norwich and Yarmouth provide rather rough representations of river craft which are our only evidence of the appearance of seventeenth-century vessels. The earliest authentic map of the city of Norwich, that made by William Cuningham in 1558, shows several small vessels berthed in the river along Quayside; they have their masts amidships and are apparently keels. Several similar craft are to be seen on Thomas Cleer's map of 1696, and on at least one of them the tiller may be clearly observed.

Three keels shown above Bishop's Bridge on Thomas Kirkpatrick's *North-East Prospect of Norwich* of 1733 are very well portrayed and give us a fairly clear idea of the appearance of such a craft at this time. The brothers Buck were a little more stylised in their representation of vessels on the river but they were usually accurate; the craft shown in their prospects of Norwich and Yarmouth seem to include both keels and wherries.

James Corbridge's map of Norwich in 1727 contains the note: "32 miles to Yarmouth. Navigable for keels of 40 or 50 Tunns. Night and day wherrys verry convenient for passengers." And Francis Blomefield's map of 1746 has much the same note. It may, perhaps rightly, be assumed from this that the wherry first came into use in East Norfolk as a passenger vessel, and certainly much documentary evidence can be produced to support this theory. Those who believe that the wherry was at this time a rowing craft and not a sailing vessel point to the craft shown in Corbridge's view of Yarmouth, obviously a passenger packet intended to make her passage as speedily as possible without regard to the strength or direction of the wind and dependent only on the muscles of a crew of hefty oarsmen.

But was this passenger vessel the same type of craft that became used for cargo carrying in succeeding years, or was it of an altogether different appearance? It is doubtful if we shall ever know for certain, but let us examine the evidence as it stands.

A passenger and goods service was in operation at least as early as the fourteenth century, for one stormy Sunday night in 1343 a certain passenger boat called the *Blitheburghosbot* carrying men and merchandise from Yarmouth towards Norwich foundered near Cantley with the loss of all but two of the forty people on board.

An East Anglian diarist has recorded for us that in 1667 one could travel from Yarmouth to Norwich for sixpence apiece, but it was not only on the Norwich River that such a service existed at that time. "There is a convenient passage by water from Beckles-Yarmouth almost every day or night, every passenger paying 4d a piece," he also noted.

Not many years later James II issued the Declaration of Indulgence and ordered all the clergy to read it in their churches. Dr. Prideaux, at that time a prebendary of

Most of the vessels shown in this detail from Corbridge's prospect of Yarmouth are keels, but steering straight for the Knowl at the junction of the North River and the Yare is a different type of craft propelled by oars. It has been suggested that this is one of the wherries or barges which carried passengers between Yarmouth and Norwich.

Norwich Cathedral, made use of the river service for secretly distributing copies of a letter, drawn up by the Earl of Halifax, persuading them not to obey this royal instruction. The account of his life, published in 1748, explains how he went about covering up his trail:

"Having made up about a dozen packets with several of these letters enclosed in each of them, he superscribed them in feigned hands, to as many Ministers in the City of Norwich; and sent a person, whom he knew he could trust, to Yarmouth, with directions to disperse them in several Wherries, which came up every night from thence to Norwich: and this being faithfully executed, the letters were delivered the next morning as directed. Now as they were sent from Yarmouth, it was generally believed that they came from Holland..."

As these wherries came up by night it seems unlikely that they were bringing passengers, though it is possible that they were small fast craft running what we would today call an express parcels service.

Palmer, in his *Perlustration of Great Yarmouth,* says that before the days of the stage coach the most commodious conveyance from Yarmouth to Norwich was by barge, which was not, however, free from danger, for in 1712 a wherry carrying passengers to Norwich was upset on Breydon and twenty persons drowned. The date of this incident is given differently by certain other writers, but Palmer's use of the terms "barge" and "wherry" is significant.

This was not the only accident to such craft in the course of the eighteenth century, for in 1782 the *Royal Charlotte* barge on its way from Yarmouth to Norwich was sunk by a sudden squall, six people losing their lives. Less than three years later "the barge" carrying passengers and goods from Yarmouth to Norwich was overset on Breydon by a sudden gust of wind, but fortunately on this occasion no lives were lost, the eighteen passengers being picked up by two keels which were passing by.

In fact the term "barge" was more often used for the passenger craft than the word "wherry." Palmer remarks that in 1809 the barge from Norwich was unable to proceed in consequence of the marshes being so flooded by a rapid thaw that the course of the river could not be followed.

When writing of a Yarmouth public house called the *Yarmouth Barge* when first licensed in 1773, because it was opposite the quay at which the barges embarked their passengers and goods, Palmer seems to draw a sharp distinction between the passenger barges and the cargo keels and wherries. "This quay was also called the Wherry Quay, because here wherries and keels took in and landed their cargoes, as the practice still is," he says.

Elsewhere, however, the same writer suggests that the words "barge" and "wherry" could indeed be synonymous. From his massive work on the history of Yarmouth comes the information that in 1725 when a coach was advertised to run every Tuesday and Friday, "Setting out at nine in the morning and making no dinner by the way", the innovation was resented by those who had always considered that "the most commodious passage between Yarmouth and Norwich was by a barge or wherry". These opponents of the coach "caused a complete barge to be built, fitted with suitable conveniences for the reception of gentlemen and ladies and others, to pass from Yarmouth to Norwich every Monday and return Tuesday, and so to pass and repass every day as occasion should require."

As further recommendation it was announced that "No fare was fixed, but it was left wholly to the generosity of the public."

The *Old Barge* public house in King Street, Norwich, is probably named after this type of passenger craft. About 1800, however, it was known as the *Three Merry Wherrymen*—and for many a year was frequented by men of that kind.

Some clue to the operations of the barges can be gained from old directories. In a 1783 directory only one barge is mentioned, running two return trips a week, and the Norwich directory of 1801, published by Thomas Peck, records that "The Old Barge goes from the Wherry Staithe, every Monday and Thursday, for Yarmouth, at ten o'clock, and returns on Tuesday and Friday. The New Barge goes from the Old Staithe, every Monday and Thursday, for Yarmouth, at ten o'clock, and returns on Tuesday and Friday."

In 1813 the barges were joined by a competitor, the first steamer on the East Coast, which was a conversion from a French privateer captured in the North Sea and sold at Yarmouth about 1811 or 1812. This 52-foot open boat, which carried 20 oars as well as three lugsails, was bought by a Yarmouth Quaker, John Wright, for £35. It seems that John and his brother Richard intended to fit her with some form of internal combustion engine using hydrogen as fuel, but they spent a considerable amount of money without achieving any success.

The name of this privateer is recorded as *L'Actif*. Perhaps this was the *Active* condemned as prize to *H.M.S. Tweed* and sold at Yarmouth in June, 1811, or perhaps she was the lugger privateer of 18 guns which had been brought in by the frigate *Nymphen* in March of the same year after being captured on her maiden voyage only a few hours after leaving Dunkirk. The privateer, mistaking the *Nymphen*, formerly a Danish frigate, for a West India ship, ran up alongside with the intention of boarding her. When the frigate opened her gunports and drew out her marines the Frenchman wisely took the hint and struck her colours.

When the internal combustion engine failed the boat was sent to the Humber under sail and taken up to Leeds, where she was fitted by Fenton, Murray and Wood with a 4 h.p. high-pressure steam engine. After being fitted out in the Leeds and Liverpool Canal basin she underwent trials on the River Aire, during which she attained a speed of less than 5 m.p.h. In later trials she proved capable of just over six against a light wind and with a full crew aboard, and used as a tug she was able to tow a sloop in ballast at just over four.

The fitting of her machinery, which had an 8 inch cylinder of 2 foot 6 inch stroke, was superintended by Mr. Richard Wright. The vessel had a cast-iron boiler.

She was insured for the sea portion of her voyage to Yarmouth on condition that the paddles were unshipped and that the engine was not worked, but when the boat was driven ashore in a gale Mr. Wright rigged up the paddles and got up steam. Taking her out to sea under power as the tide refloated her, he continued his journey to Yarmouth under sail. He lost his insurance, but saved the boat.

A Yarmouth-Norwich paddle steamer of about 1830, the *Emperor*, as depicted in an engraving after a painting by James Stark.

The *Experiment,* as she was renamed, arrived at Yarmouth on July 19th 1813, and on August 9th Sir Edmund and Lady Bacon and their family, with other local notabilities, had a trip to Breydon. Thousands of spectators stood by the quay to watch her go through Yarmouth bridge. The same day the Public Crier went round the streets of Norwich announcing that the new steam barge was to pass Thorpe at half past five that afternoon, and the banks of the Wensum were lined with spectators until late in the evening, when it dawned on the crowds that they had been hoaxed. Many of them saw the vessel arrive at what was then called Sandling's Ferry, now Pull's Ferry, the following afternoon after a 5½-hour trip.

An advertisement appeared in both the Norwich newspapers* respectfully informing people "that the STEAM PACKET will regularly leave Turner's Bowling-Green, Yarmouth, at seven o'clock every morning, and leave Norwich every afternoon precisely at 3 o'clock." In the *Chronicle* appeared the additional information that from Norwich to Yarmouth the fare was 4s. 6d.; for six miles it was 1s., for 12 miles 2s., for 18 miles 3s. and for 24 miles 4s. These prices applied to the fore cabin, fares for the after cabin and for children under ten being half.

The *Chronicle's* description of the new steamer is somewhat amusing. "Its principle of motion is a number of oars, something in the shape of a barn shovel; these are fixed in an axis forming a sort of water wheel, one on each side of the vessel, which are turned by machinery that is put in motion by a small steam engine. Its rate of going was about 5 miles in the hour; it seems likely to be a safe and convenient mode of conveyance to and from Yarmouth, and if the proprietor can get it to act in a manner so as to establish the certainty of its arrival, little doubt can be entertained but it will answer his purpose, as few people will regard the splashing of the oars, or the noise of the machinery."

The steam barge, as the newspapers insisted on calling the *Experiment,* served a most useful purpose in keeping the river open for other craft during the first two weeks of 1814, but the very severe winter, described at the time as "almost Russian", won in the end and the Yare was frozen over, bringing the steam-boat services to an end for a time.

About this time there was building at Yarmouth another steamer, the *Orwell,* which was intended to provide a service between Harwich and Ipswich. Her builder was a shipwright by the name of James Lepingwell, who was later concerned in the building of other steamers, and her engine was produced in the Norwich foundry of Aggs and Curr. Unfortunately that engine, undoubtedly the first marine engine built in Norfolk, proved unequal to the task of propelling the little vessel and another engine built in London was brought by sea to Yarmouth for fitting into the *Orwell.*

The vessel did not arrive at Ipswich until August, 1815. She operated on the river between Ipswich and Harwich for a few weeks, but then was withdrawn, never, so far as can be discovered, to reappear.

* *The Norwich Mercury* and the *Norfolk Chronicle.*

Another Yarmouth-built steamer of which little is known was the *Eagle,* a curious double-hulled vessel which, according to a reference in a Parliamentary report of 1822, went up the Seine soon after her building in 1815. If she did in fact go to France she later returned to the East Coast, for she was advertised for sale at Yarmouth in 1817, when she was described as being 59 feet long and measuring 50 tons, "with steam engine and apparatus complete, having two stern posts and two keels, with a water paddle in the midships..."

Other early steamers built at Yarmouth were the *Phoenix,* a 25-ton vessel with a 4 h.p. high pressure engine, and the *Richmond,* a 60-tonner built by Lepingwell for the Thames river service between London and Richmond. The *Defiance,* according to Kennedy's *Records of the Early British Steamships* built at Yarmouth by Wright in 1816, was the first steamer in Holland.

The Norwich-Yarmouth steam packet was next advertised in the local papers in April, 1814, when it was announced that she would set off from Foundry Bridge, Norwich, on Easter Sunday and return from Yarmouth the same day. On Mondays, Wednesdays and Fridays she was to sail from Norwich, making the return voyage on Tuesdays, Thursdays and Saturdays.

The *Experiment* was soon joined by a second packet, for when Yarmouth Races were held in August, 1814, it was stated in local papers that the New Steam Packet would start from the *Old Barge* public house in King Street, Norwich. The *Norfolk Chronicle's* Yarmouth correspondent recorded that "Our races this week attracted a very large assemblage of company ... upwards of five hundred persons came from Norwich in the Steam Packets and Barge ..."

It is worthy of note that the Barge was still running in spite of the competition of the steamers. The barges had been carrying passengers between city and coast for many years, and they do not seem to have disappeared finally until the coming of the railways in the 1840s.

For a time the two packets left on alternate days, providing a daily return service between Norwich and Yarmouth, but in October, 1814, the *Mercury* announced that the new steam barge had taken to leaving King Street at the same time as the original one left Foundry Bridge.

Advertisements of 1815 mention the *Hope* steam packet, owned by T. Hannent and Co., apparently a rival to the packets run by Wright and presumably the vessel which had begun running the previous year. Unhappily the newspapers rarely mention the vessels by name and it is difficult to determine which vessel is being referred to in many instances.

A timber-laden keel at Norwich shown in an engraving after a painting by James Stark.

For this reason it has proved impossible so far to trace the story of the packets in any detail, although it is clear from another source that about 1814 Wright had a new packet, the *Telegraph,* built at Yarmouth and fitted with a 10 h.p. engine. Soon after building the *Telegraph* Wright replaced the *Experiment* by another new vessel, the *Courier,* into which was put the *Experiment's* machinery.

It was not long before Wright decided to test the sea-keeping qualities of his boats, and the *Telegraph* was sent to the Medway to run between Sheerness and Chatham. She was not powerful enough to be a success on this service, however, and so returned after a few weeks to Yarmouth. When she arrived home it was found that the use of salt water in the boiler had ruined it, and in the course of extensive repairs a new cast-iron end was bolted on to the old wrought-iron boiler.

A brief report in the *Norfolk Chronicle* in November, 1816, records that the *Lord Nelson* steam packet had made the voyage from Norwich to Yarmouth in only 3 hours

34 minutes. This new packet, whose proper name seems to have been *Nelson,* was owned by Thomas Watts, of Norwich.

The *Telegraph* was involved in one of the worst disasters ever to occur on the Norfolk rivers. On the morning of Good Friday, 1817, the rival packets, Wright's *Telegraph* and Watts' *Nelson,* were at their moorings near Foundry Bridge, anxious to be off. Wright's got away first, and had given three snorts of her high-pressure machinery when with a roar the cast-iron end of her boiler shattered. The boiler tore itself loose from its bed and hurled itself out through the stern like an enormous rocket.

It seems that the cast-iron end put on after the *Telegraph's* sea trip had given way, probably owing to the engineer having hung weights on the safety valve to boost more speed than her rival. Of the 22 people on board nine were killed and six seriously injured, two of whom died later. One of the first people to step aboard (he afterwards served on the inquest jury) saw the corpse of the sister from whom he had parted only a few minutes before. Under a seat in the forepart of the packet was found a young child asleep; another, less fortunate, had been blown into the river and drowned. One man who had been standing above the boiler was blown up in the air and came down unhurt! A militia sergeant proceeding to Yarmouth coolly changed to Watts' boat and continued his journey.

"Notwithstanding this shocking catastrophe, the other steam packets were full of passengers on Monday," a note in the *Cambridge Chronicle* tells us.

This accident led to the setting up by Parliament of a Select Committee to consider means of preventing similar explosions. In their report it was stated that "it appears to this committee, from the evidence of several experienced engineers, examined before them, that the explosion in the steam packet at Norwich was caused not only by the improper construction and materials of the boiler but the safety valve connected with it having been overloaded..." The Committee recommended that boilers should in future be made of wrought iron, that they should be provided with two safety valves and that they should be subject to the inspection of a qualified engineer.

Other people also put forward their favourite ideas. One correspondent suggested the propriety of placing the engine in a separate boat which would tow the passenger craft. More practically, a fund was raised for the relief of the sufferers; John Wright himself is said to have lost £10,000 through having to pay compensation.

Anticipating that many people would be frightened of travelling in steam packets, Wright converted his other vessel, the *Courier,* into a horse packet. The steam machinery was taken out and replaced by a platform 18 feet in diameter round which walked four horses, turning an upright shaft from which power was transmitted to the paddleshaft through a bevel wheel. The horses were changed half way, presumably at Reedham.

About a year after its conversion the *Courier* was sold to Tuck and Fisher, a Yarmouth firm of plumbers, who continued to run the horse packet for several years. The *Courier* was eventually converted back to steam power, however.

The *Courier* was not the first vessel using horse power to be seen in Yarmouth harbour, for a horse-powered dredger had been at work in the harbour since about 1793. This "Didelling Engine", as it was locally known, was driven by two horses working in the same manner as in a horse mill. They turned machinery which raised eight iron baskets, capable of dredging 220 tons of mud a day.

The horse packet came into use within a few weeks of the disaster, but Watts decided to keep his packet running as a steamer. He announced in July, 1817, that the *Nelson* had been inspected by Charles Harvey, M.P. for Norwich and chairman of the Select Committee, and that he had his authority for stating that it was constructed in every way in accordance with the Select Committee's recommendations. The machinery was a low pressure condensing engine, and the wrought-iron boiler was fitted with the requisite two safety valves.

The boiler of this steamer did give way two years later owing to corrosion, but without the serious consequences of the bursting of the *Telegraph*'s high pressure boiler. The *Nelson* was rebuilt and reboilered and then returned to service.

The building of the railway from Yarmouth to Norwich in the early 1840's made the steam packets redundant, even if it did lead to a slight shortening of the distance between the two places by river through the building of the New Cut at Thorpe St. Andrew, a short way below the city. In the mid-1840s, however, the steam packets *British Queen, Emperor, Sovereign* and *Dahlia,* the latter built of iron, were still maintaining a service between city and seaport, though in 1844 a local newspaper reported that "about 60 cwt. of tea and coffee have been brought to Norwich by the Yarmouth and Norwich Railway Company...", adding prophetically "We should not be surprised if that practice became more general in busy weeks, particularly when the wind is contrary for the favourable transit of the wherries."

Some of the steam-boat proprietors were already realising that the future lay with what we would term the tripper trade, and as early as 1843 one was advertising that the *Tickler* steam packet, "capable of conveying from one to two hundred passengers", might be hired by pleasure parties for summer trips on the river. Earlier she had been running an almost daily service from Norwich to Yarmouth and back, leaving Norwich quite early in the morning and returning in the afternoon.

One of these packets, the *Victoria*, built at Norwich by Blyth and Son in 1837, was said to be able to "consume her own smoke, which will be a great recommendation to the passengers going by her." The engine was also built in Norwich, by Blyth and Francis, but unhappily it is not recorded how she was to "consume her own smoke".

These packets were quite large vessels, another built about the same time, "of prime English oak, being 80 foot long, 11 foot 6 inches in beam, with very broad plankways", yet drawing only 3 foot.

By the 1850s it appears that the railway had taken over the scheduled services from the packets, but the steamers continued to find employment on pleasure trips for many years to come. One of the best-remembered steamers on the Yare was the *Jenny Lind,* a clinker-built steamer launched from Hall's yard at Reedham in 1879, which ran a popular service between Norwich and Bramerton Woods End. Just as well remembered as the *Jenny Lind* is a Norwich character nicknamed Billy Bluelight who would endeavour to walk, or run, from Norwich by road and reach Bramerton in time to greet the steamer.

So much for the passenger vessels. What of the cargo carriers? By the 1780s the wherry had developed into substantially the type of vessel that was known on the rivers of Norfolk until the middle of the twentieth century, and was even then beginning to supersede the less handy keel.

In Norwich Castle Museum is a horn cup, on one side of which is a carefully drawn profile picture of a wherry. Above is the inscription "Success to the Happy Return,"

The keelman's wife, baby in arms, in the scuttle of a keel's cabin.

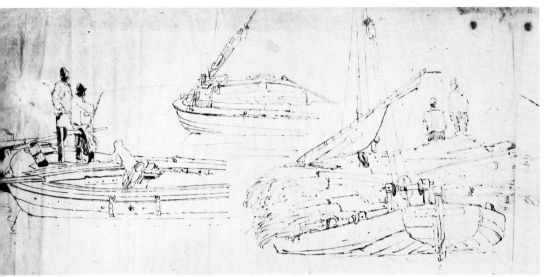

A keel laden with reeds, and sketches of the bow and stern of a keel; drawings probably made about 1820–1840.

which apparently was the name of the wherry, and on the left is the figure of a man in jacket and petticoat, carrying a stick, and on the right is the figure of a woman. On the other side of the cup is the inscription "Robert and Mary Adkins, Irstead. September 12th, 1789".

This must be one of the earliest detailed pictures of such a craft, and is certainly the best of early pictures. The wherry is very much like the later vessels, but there are some differences. The sail has four rows of reef points, and the system of spans seems less complicated than in later craft—though the latter may be due to the simplicity of the drawing; there is no winch, and only one pair of timberheads forward instead of the two pairs found in later craft. The bow is raking, but not curved as some artists showed the bows of wherries, possibly erroneously.

The fact that some artists insisted on drawing wherries with very decidedly curved stems even in the middle of the present century, when no wherry afloat was in fact in any way apple-bowed, causes one to doubt the authenticity of some old pictures. Certain artists have illustrated wherries which appear even to be swim-headed, but it is extremely doubtful if such a wherry ever did exist.

Another horn cup in the same museum shows two vessels, apparently a keel and a wherry, passing under Greyfriars Bridge, one of the half-dozen which spanned the

Wensum in the middle of Norwich. A perspective view instead of a profile, it does not appear to be such an accurately and carefully made representation of the vessels as the first.

The *Norwich Gazette* in 1727 carried an advertisement for two wherries, "of about 8 Tuns Burden ... with all the Tackel, Masts, Sails, Ropes, Tilts, Hoops and Oars..." and this and later advertisements, together with the picture of the *Happy Return,* present us with a most valuable idea of what a wherry of that time was like. In 1781 the wherry *Buckenham,* drawing only 2 foot 6 inches, was to be sold at Aylsham, and in the same year the *William and Mary,* drawing 2 foot 10 inches, and carrying 12 tons of coals, was to be sold at Horning *Swan.* Next year a hatched wherry, about five years old and of 15 tons, called the *Fortitude* was to be sold or let. Mr. Walter Rye, who turned up this advertisement during his researches into Norfolk history, remarked that he was inclined to think that hitherto these craft had not been fitted with hatches. From the specific mention of hatches in this and other advertisements of about the same time one may judge he was probably correct.

These were very small vessels, probably no more than about 30 foot long, but it is likely that the wherries operating on the Norwich River were even then rather larger

An early nineteenth century wherry in use as a dredger about 1890. Her length of about 35 feet, and her raking stem and transom stern, mark her as a survivor from an earlier era.

than this. When a Yarmouth boatbuilder died in 1779 local newspapers printed an advertisement of the sale of "a large new built Wherry, built with English Oak Board, which will be finished in about ten or 12 days ... She is 51 feet long and 13 wide, supposing to carry 20 Chaldron of coals."

The keels, on the other hand, carried much more cargo. Both the keel *Hand and Hand,* for sale at Norwich in February, 1779, and the "hatch keel" *John and Joseph,* for sale at Coltishall later the same year, were said to be of about 50 tons burthen. The biggest recorded keel, the *Success,* was of no less than 97 tons burthen.

A description of a keel is given in *A Concise History and Directory of the City of Norwich for 1811* printed by and for C. Berry, jun. in 1810. "The keels and wherries which navigate between Norwich and Yarmouth are acknowledged to be superior to any other small craft in England, for carrying a larger burthen, and being worked at a smaller expense;— their burthen is from fifteen and fifty tons; they have but one mast, which lets down, and carry only one large square sail, are covered close by hatches, and have a cabin superior to many coasting vessels, in which oftentimes the keelman and his family live; they require only two persons to navigate them and sometimes perform their passage (thirty-two miles) in five hours."

Nearly 20 years later, in *A Norfolk Tour*, it is remarked that "The general navigation from Norwich to Yarmouth is performed by keels and wherries; the former are chiefly restricted to the freightage of timber and are far less numerous than formerly; the wherries are peculiar to the rivers of Norfolk and Suffolk, and those made use of on the Wensum carry from fifteen to forty tons, and draw from three to four feet of water; the mast is by the head, and is so balanced, by means of lead, that the strength of one man is sufficient to raise or lower it in the event of passing bridges; on this, by the action of a windlass, the sail is hoisted, being extended by a gaff at the upper edge. These vessels are seldom navigated by more than two hands, and one of them is often a boy, or the wife of the waterman; in the latter case it is not infrequent for them to have their families in a cabin placed at the stern."

This description seems to have been part of the stock-in-trade of directory compilers, for it appears in several different nineteenth-century publications with little or no alteration.

Some of the keels seem, from their tonnage, to have been pretty big craft, but what we know today of the keels is based mainly on an example which, after being used by J. S. Hobrough & Son for dredging work, was sunk at Whitlingham to help hold the bank up. In what must have been a relatively early example of marine archaeological excavation, the vessel was disinterred in 1912 so that measurements could be taken for the building of a model. She had an overall length of 55 foot and a beam amidships of 13 foot 8 inches. The depth amidships was only 4 foot, increasing to 4 foot 10 inches at the after beam.

The mast, unlike that of a wherry, was a light spar and the tabernacle in which it was stepped did not require the massive knees which supported the wherry's. There were winches fore and aft, that in the bows being for raising the mast, through a hefty tackle, and that in the stern being for the halyard. The mast was stayed by a single shroud each side, and there was also a tackle from the masthead leading aft which seems to have served as a backstay and as a downhaul when it was necessary to lower the mast.

The yard was hooked to a traveller similar to that found on the lug-rigged fishing boats of Norfolk and Suffolk.

The cabin in which the keelman and his family lived was in the bow, generally with a scuttle on the starboard side, as can be seen in paintings and drawings of this type of craft. It is generally said that the keel had a transom stern; certainly the one dug up at Whitlingham had this form of construction and so did many others, but it seems that just as some wherries had transoms some keels may well have been double-ended.

The drawings which illustrate this section are of unknown origin; they illustrate very well some features of the keels. Probably made about 1820-1840, they are rather rough sketches in brown ink on tracing paper. In one of them the keelman's wife can be seen in the cabin scuttle, holding the baby in her arms—an interesting sidelight on the domestic arrangements of the keelmen.

The last of the keels, her mast taken out, was used in dredging operations by James Hobrough & Son in the 1890s.

CHAPTER FOUR

The Waterborne Cargoes

WHERRIES carried a great variety of cargoes in the days when water transport was at worst the cheapest and speediest means of conveyance for heavy goods. In fact a list of the things they carried would be almost a complete list of the goods in which trade was carried on in Norfolk. The manufacturers of Norwich depended on the keels and wherries for sending away their products, and the tradesmen of the city and of smaller market towns depended on them for a supply of merchandise before the coming of the railways and of speedy, convenient road transport.

The diversity of cargoes carried on the Norfolk rivers can be judged by the list of tolls levied under the Tonnage Act of 1726 for repairing the walls, gates and other public works of Norwich. "And whereas the said walls, gates, bridges, wastes, stathes, and wharfs are now become very ruinous and out of repair ... there shall be paid by every master or other person having the command, rule, management or working of any boat, keel, wherry, lighter, hoy, or other vessel which shall pass up the common river higher than Thorp Hall, in Thorp next Norwich, towards the said city of Norwich, before they shall unlade any goods or merchandises therein, the tolls or duties hereinafter mentioned."

After listing coals, wheat, rye, barley, malt and other grain, salt, sugar, tobacco, molasses and other dry goods, the Act speaks of such miscellaneous articles as rope, Smyrna raisins, oil, pitch, tar, nails, bars of iron, millstones, grindstones, pantiles, building stone; hardly anything is missing. Timber of various kinds, single and double deals, dairy products such as butter and cheese, everything under the sun seemed to be listed, and doubtless the Corporation filled its coffers from this source.

"Norwich adds greatly to the trade of Yarmouth, by the importation of about 40,000 chaldrons of coal yearly," we read in 1810; "Wine, fish, oil, Irish yarn, and all heavy goods which come from thence by the River Yare; and in peace the exportation of its manufactures to Russia, Germany, Holland, Denmark, Norway, Spain, Portugal, Italy & c."

It was not only the merchants and manufacturers who benefited from water transport, however. The rivers were just as important to the agricultural economy of Norfolk and Suffolk, as is revealed by Bacon's *Report on the Agriculture of Norfolk* of 1844. "A large portion of the corn, barley, malt, etc. of the eastern districts is conveyed to Yarmouth, Beccles etc. for exportation at about 1s. 9d. to 2s. per ton, or 3d. per coomb, in vessels called wherries. These vessels on their return from the ports bring marl, manure (artificial or natural), oil cake, coal etc; in short, most of the natural products agriculture can require, at an equally cheap rate—in some places to the door of the farmer, while at other points the marl is laid up on staithes or wharves until required for use. This manure is most important, as a large part of the extreme Eastern district having no marl or chalk, is thus enabled to secure a very important adjunct at a cost cheap in comparison with what its carriage would be by land. Rushes and course hay grown on the marshes adjacent are also carried in large flat-bottomed boats to staithes where waggons take them to the farmyard."

An earlier inquiry into the rural economy of the county, made by Marshall in 1787, underlined the importance of the marl trade. "Before the use of marl (which has not been brought by water, I apprehend, above ten or fifteen years) the farmers could grow no turneps; the land letting for ten or twelve shillings an acre: now, the turneps upon it are remarkably fine; and the land lets at full twenty shillings an acre; a rent the occupiers could not pay, were it not for marl."

Cheap transport by river played an essential part, for Marshall adds: "The distance between Wood-Bastwick and the marl pits at Thorpe next Norwich is not, by land, more than six or seven miles; yet the farmers find it cheaper to fetch their marl fifty miles by water, and then carry it, perhaps, half a mile from the staith to the ground, than fetch it the six or seven miles by land."

It seems strange that marl had to be taken all that way from the Thorpe pits, for there were other sources of marl which one would have thought were more conveniently situated for farmers at Woodbastwick and other places on the North River. The chief of them were the enormous marl workings at Horstead, where the chalk sloped gently down to the level of the Bure. The riverside quarries developed at the beginning of the nineteenth century were extended in time into the hill slopes, a channel being cut to give small wherries direct access to the working face. For more than half a century this area just to the north of Wroxham Hall presented a picture of great industry, the white slopes looming clean above the laden wherries.

The workings became so extensive over the course of years that in one place wherries were able to voyage for at least half a mile into the hillside to load chalk, which they carried not only to farms needing marl for top dressing the fields but to nearby lime kilns and to the cement works downriver.

Writing of the Horstead marlpits in 1948, that eminent East Anglian geologist J. E. Sainty told how they became known to the scientific world for fossils, attracting the attention even of the great Sir Charles Lyell, who in 1825 travelled to Horstead and "visited an extensive range of quarries on the River Bure which afforded a continuous section a quarter of a mile in length of white chalk exposed to a depth of 26

One of the canals at Horstead by which marl was lightered from the deep pits known as Little Switzerland.

A reed barge with cross beams fore and aft. The drainage mill in the background is Hunsett Mill, on the Ant above Wayford Bridge.

feet and covered by a thick bed of gravel." Five years before, the skeleton of a mastodon had been found lying on its side in the gravel, but by the time geologists arrived "the whole had been carried away with the chalk and burnt for lime or spread in minute fragments over the fields." One wonders what Norfolk field was fertilised by this "grandfather of all the elephants."

The name by which these cuttings became known in the locality, Little Switzerland, gives an idea of the size of the workings, from which many thousands of tons of material must have been dug and carted away. When the last pit closed somewhere about 1875 and the fir trees planted on the slopes began to reach maturity the scenery really began to fit the name.

Another kind of dressing for the land was manufactured at a factory on the banks of the Bure just outside Yarmouth, namely artificial manure. Wherries were employed bringing the raw material from ships in Yarmouth harbour, and this was an unpopular job for several reasons. It was a foul-smelling cargo, from which corrosive acid drained into the bilges, and wherries employed in this trade sometimes had to lie aground beside the factory; a bad berth meant a strained wherry.

There was also a fertiliser factory at Haddiscoe. The proprietors, G. & J. Bagshaw, did not possess any wherries, but they frequently hired some for conveying their products. Placed as it was, with the Waveney on the north side and the Great Eastern Railway on the south, this factory had no reason to complain of lack of transport facilities, but it closed during the years of depression and was gutted by fire in 1935.

The importance to the agricultural community of the muck, marl and similar materials carried by river is shown by the freedom from toll enjoyed by cargoes intended for the improvement of farmland under the Act of Parliament for making the Bure navigable to Aylsham, but this was far from being the full extent of agriculture's dependence on water transport. All kinds of produce went by wherry, and many an estate which lay convenient to one of the rivers was served by small cuts made for the purpose of carrying corn to the markets and freighting back manure and marl for improving the land.

The wherry *Lady Violet* was built for Lord Beauchamp, of Langley Hall, who used her solely for transporting the coal and goods required for his estate and for conveying the produce of his farms. She was said to have been constructed from oaks felled in Langley Park, and was named after Lady Beauchamp.

In the last century, when horse transport in Norwich and other towns meant a big demand for hay, wherries could be seen sailing along with that commodity stacked high above their decks, and often overhanging the sides as well. One has only to look at the paintings of the Norwich School to find out what this looked like, for such floating haystacks seem to have been popular subjects with some of Crome's followers.

Like the stackie barges of the Thames Estuary, many of these fodder-carrying wherries returned to the farms with "muck", the sweepings of the streets and the clearings of the stables. While the stable litter of Norwich and such inland centres might consist largely of straw of one kind and another, that carried by wherries from Yarmouth was of a different but no less beneficial kind. Yarmouth being surrounded by marshes and the sea, straw was a scarce and expensive article in the town, so the stables were littered with sea-sand instead. As the bed became soiled or wet fresh sand was scattered on the floor until the whole was saturated with dung and "a muck of singular excellence" was produced. Another manure carried by wherry from Yarmouth was fish; when there was a glut many of the fishing fleet found it impossible to sell their catches except at a very low price for spreading on the fields.

Stable sand was not the only kind of sand carried by river from Yarmouth, however. There was a very convenient shoal near the harbour mouth at Gorleston, a kind of fairy's purse, which provided a constant supply of sea sand such as was in demand for spreading on the floors of houses in the old days. One wherry which used to engage in the sand trade was the *Adam and Eve*, owned by a Mrs. Howes, who kept the *Adam and Eve* public house in the parish of St. Helen, Norwich, one of the city's old watermen's pubs.

The Corporation of Great Yarmouth made capital out of a similar magic pocket from which 20,000 to 25,000 tons of ballast was dug each year. As much as 300 tons was sometimes excavated during the course of a single ebb, being loaded into ballast keels and taken to ships in the harbour which required ballast after unloading cargo, and the Corporation, which claimed the exclusive right of ballasting vessels using the port, found this to be a profitable business, especially as the sea filled up the quite extensive excavations tide after tide.

The reeds so widely used for thatching in the eastern parts of Norfolk and Suffolk provided many a freight for wherries. Cut from the margins of the rivers and broads and from the extensive reed beds of such areas as Woodbastwick Fen, the reeds were usually carried to a convenient staithe by the reed barges from which the reed cutters worked. These broad shallow vessels had a saucer-like hull which was in many ways not entirely unlike that of a wherry, though considerably smaller and shallower. Normally tarred both inside and out, most of these craft were completely open, with no cross-beams to interfere with loading and unloading. Large numbers of frames some two inches square were used to compensate for the lack of any tie-beam, and these were set about fifteen inches apart. The sides were of three-quarter-inch oak strakes.

The reed lighters were most often quanted along the dykes, but the loading of a high stack of reed bundles made it awkward to use a quant efficiently in open water and they were frequently rowed by a man stationed right up in the bows, tholes being set up for this purpose.

According to size, these craft were classified as whole, three-quarter or half-load boats. The whole-load boats, about 25 foot long and 8 foot to 9 foot in beam, would carry two cart-loads of reed.

When it came to carrying reeds over longer distances, however, it was the wherry that was called on to do the job. In 1953 E. A. Ellis, the Norfolk naturalist, noted that a wherry could carry more than 2,300 bunches, amounting to something near 390 fathom, of closely packed thatching reed. The bundles of reed were expertly stowed and fitted in snugly. This large load could be carried because it was allowed to overhang the right-ups and spread across the plankways. It was a motor wherry Mr. Ellis saw at this work, and the waterman would have little cause to use the quant except to give the wherry a set off from the bank each time he moved on from one reed stack to another, but even in the days of sail the method of loading was the same.

Hay and marsh litter were among the cargoes which went by water in the old days. When a cargo of this kind was stacked high above the right-ups so that a wherry resembled a floating haystack with a sail it was necessary for the mate to con the vessel from atop the stack as the skipper at the helm could not see ahead.

Even garden produce found its way to market by wherry at one time, just as the produce of the Dutch polders is today taken to the auction centres by canal boat, and at least one wherry, the *Little Georgie,* seems to have earned the soubriquet " the cabbage wherry". This nickname fitted her well, for she was owned by a Ludham market gardener named George Griffen. She was a very small wherry, but it is recorded that Griffen, who used to sail her to Yarmouth himself, was no midget; he stood over six feet tall, and always wore a round skin hat. He and his wherry were eagerly awaited by the youngsters on the North Quay at Yarmouth, it is said, because their reward for helping to unload the cargo of cabbages, turnips, cauliflowers and potatoes was usually a carrot or swede which was quickly devoured by the hungry children.

Another market wherry was the 20-ton *Rob Roy,* owned and sailed by John Anderson, of Reedham. Each Wednesday and Saturday she was boarded at Reedham quay by women and children with their peds of vegetables and baskets of butter and farm produce destined to be sold in Yarmouth market place. After the seven or eight-mile trip downriver they would land at Burton's Quay at Yarmouth and take refreshment at the adjoining tavern, kept by Benjamin Burton, hence the name of the quay, before making off up the rows to the market place.

The carriage of corn, barley, malt and similar cargoes has already been mentioned. Some wherries carried little else, for many millers and corn dealers possessed their own wherry or even a small fleet. Horace Gambling, of Buxton Mills, between Coltishall and Aylsham, is mentioned in a later chapter; George Robertson, of South Walsham, appeared in a directory of 1864 as corn and coal merchant and wherry owner, and so did John Parker at Burgh St. Peter on the Waveney. In later years Press Bros. of North Walsham, to become successively Press and Pallett and Pallett, Barclay & Co., Woods, Sadd, Moore & Co. of Loddon, and W. D. & A. E. Walker, of Bungay, all of them in the corn or malt trade, owned their own fleets of wherries.

There were watermills on the upper reaches of the Waveney, the Bure and the Ant, and windmills in nearly every village, while many places also had maltings. Besides the big maltings at Norwich, Southtown and other such centres there were smaller maltings at such places as Reedham, Panxworth, Salhouse, Wayford Bridge and North Walsham. Most of these were erected close by the river or at the head of a convenient dyke and depended largely, if not entirely, on water transport.

Horning maltings stood on the staithe, where there is now an open space. Unlike the later malthouses, with their blank red-brick walls, the Horning maltings presented a mosaic of flint and Surlingham brick and even contained relics of St. Benet's Abbey,

The malthouses on the quay at Horning. Both wherries in the photograph are pleasure wherries, but trading wherries used to lie there to load from the maltings.

which had provided material for many a building in the area. This range of buildings was once used as a factory for the manufacture of biscuits for the Navy during the Crimean War and afterwards became a crepe factory before being adapted for the malting process when the production of barley increased locally during the second half of the nineteenth century.

Much of the malt from these maltings, large and small, went to Norwich by wherry to be used in the city's several breweries. Though some brewing firms depended on chartered craft, Steward and Patteson owned both sailing wherries and a small steamer, the *Annie,* which they had built at Yarmouth in 1899, and used them for distributing their ales to riverside pubs and for carrying beer to Yarmouth for shipment further afield.

After brewing, when the liquid had been drawn off, the drains of the malt or hops that remained were collected by farmers for use as cattle fodder, most of them sending their waggons to the breweries to collect the cheap and useful waste. Some of it went by river, however, and one wherry owned by a Waveney valley farmer used to make two trips a week from the farm to Bullard's brewery at Norwich to fetch such cargoes. The master of this wherry, one Bradley, was well known for his disinclination to use the quant more than absolutely necessary. Many times he brought his wherry from the iron railway bridge at Trowse to the brewery in St. Miles's without once using his quant, no small feat in view of the number of bridges to be passed and the difficulties of navigation in this part of the river.

Stone for the roads, stone for building, and stone for the river walls, chalk for lime-burning and chalk and mud for cement manufacturing were all carried by river in the nineteenth century. At the end of Long Reach, Thorpe, wherries used to load chalk from pits at Whitlingham, and on the Trowse side of the river was one of the many lime kilns which in those days poured forth acrid smoke into the riverside air, while near Bishop's Bridge at Norwich were two wooden tips from which wherries used to load stone from stonepits on Plumstead Road. Six or eight tumblers (tumbrils) would come down at a time, and as they carried nearly a ton apiece a wherry would be loaded in a day.

For unloading stone and similar cargoes the wherryman used a barrow of unusual design, the most conspicuous point about it being the absence of shafts or legs, the latter being omitted so that the barrow could be rested on the eleven-inch wide planks which every wherry carried. The handle and side was cut out of a single piece of $1\frac{1}{4}$in. wood, and after the two ends and the bottom had been fixed in position the sides were bolted together by four 5/16th inch bars which had large square washers and nuts on the outer ends, holding the barrow very rigidly together. In addition the top and bottom of the sides were strengthened by iron bands and the two ends had strips of

Loading wherries at the tips just below Bishop's Bridge, Norwich. One of the shifting right-ups of the first wherry has been removed.

iron on their top edges, these irons being extended and fixed to the sides. The inch-thick bottom boards were supported by transverse bearers whose ends passed through the sides of the barrow and were given additional support by U-shaped iron brackets nailed on the outer side. Their heavy and robust construction was an insurance against damage should the wherryman slip or accidentally wheel the barrow off the plank linking wherry and staithe.

Two 22 foot deals were included in the normal equipment of every wherry, along with two quarter deals 16 foot long which were just of the right length to place across the hold. A man working on the floor of the hold with a shovel had a long way to "hull" cargo into a barrow on a plank with both ends on the standing right-ups, so to bring it within reach one end would be placed on the right-up and the other held by a right-up iron, a bracket hooking on the inside of the coamings.

Bricks and tiles formed frequent cargoes, some wherries being owned by the local brickmakers and being used almost exclusively for the carriage of their products, thus earning the nickname of "The Brick Hod" in some instances. Riverside brickworks large and small played a big part in the economy of the area at one time, their products being seen in the marsh farmhouses, the windmills and the barns as well as in the houses and cottages of the towns and villages.

Two of the brickyards served by river transport were to be found at Surlingham, one being above the ferry and the other near Coldham Hall. One of the Surlingham brickmakers owned his own wherries, the *Meteor* and the *Herald*.

From here were shipped the bricks for the building of Woodbastwick Hall as well as those for many of the houses and commercial premises of Yarmouth. One wherryman employed in these wherries has told how a load of bricks was eight and a half thousand, the payment received being 3s. 6d. a thousand, for which he and his mate had to load the wherry at the brickyard and unload and stack the bricks on the quay at Yarmouth.

The brickyard at Rockland, not far downriver, was also served by wherry, the kilns being at the head of a short dyke with a T-shaped head in which wherries could turn. A similar dyke in the same vicinity led to a coal bin where coal brought by wherry from Yarmouth was unloaded for distribution in the neighbouring villages. This

Wherries lying at the Burgh Castle cement works in the 1880s.

brickworks was at one time owned by a man named Rudd, who had three wherries, the *Providence, Ego* and another. Later owners were a Norwich firm of builders' merchants, Lacey & Lincoln, who had a number of wherries including the *Rockland Trader, Emily* and *Our Boys*. This works closed down during the 1939-45 war because, it is said, the glare of the fire in the kiln was too conspicuous during the blackout.

Other brickfields on the southern rivers served by wherry were at and near Reedham, at Burgh Castle, Herringfleet, Somerleyton, Oulton Broad and Beccles. The wherry *Widgeon* was built at Wroxham by H. Press for Mr. Green's brickyard in the same parish, and other North River brickfields included one at Martham from which bricks were taken in the last century for the building of some of Yarmouth's seafront hotels.

At Burgh Castle, near the Roman fortress looking out over the confluence of the Waveney and the Yare, there was besides the brickyard a cement works which sent numerous cargoes away by wherry during the latter part of the century. There was usually a line of wherries along the river bank by the smoking kilns, for the raw material came by water, just as the product left the works aboard wherries, a number of which belonged to the proprietors of the works. This cement factory does not seem to have had a very long life, for it was built in 1859 and closed before the end of the century.

There was another cement factory at Berney Arms on the north bank of the Yare within sight of Burgh Castle. The lofty windmill which still stands like a sentinel in that lonely spot did more than pump water off the marshes in those days; it ground cement clinker for the Reedham Cement Works, as the factory was known, the vertical stones being situated on the second floor of the 70 foot brick tower. Just when that mill was built, by Stolworthy, the Yarmouth millwright, nobody seems able to say, but it was there in 1860 when the Reedham Cement Works was to let; it was said in the advertisement that the mill, with its patent sails, was twice as powerful as the 12 h.p. steam engine which powered another part of the factory, and it stood for many a year after the works closed in 1880. It did a useful job of clearing water from the marshland dykes until after the second world war, when electric pumps took over; as most of the marsh mills followed the wherries into oblivion Berney Arms Mill was transferred by the Lower Bure, Halvergate Fleet and Acle Marshes Internal Drainage Board to the Ministry of Works in 1951 for preservation as an historic monument.

Fuel for these cement works had to be brought in by wherry, of course. One of the most essential trades carried on by river was that in coal, which was taken from the colliers lying in Yarmouth harbour to merchants all over the district. Much of it was needed by Norwich gasworks and by the city's coal merchants. Many a local coal merchant owned his own wherries; at Norwich W. England had the *Gem* and the *Leveret* as well as his coalyard near Fye Bridge, and at Upton on the North River John

Unloading coal from the *Meteor,* one of the wherries owned at Surlingham brickyard.

Helsdon in the 1860s was both wherry owner and coal dealer, as was Joseph Powley at Tunstall, to mention but three.

A good deal of timber was carried on the Norfolk rivers, both locally felled logs and imported sawn timber being among the cargoes. When the last few keels were considered no longer fit for the carriage of anything better their hatches were left off altogether and they carried timber until at last they were superseded even for that trade; one of James Stark's plates in *River Scenery of Norfolk and Suffolk* shows a keel with a load of heavy logs piled high above the right-ups. It may have been that the square sail of a keel did not foul such a cargo as easily as the gaff sail of a wherry.

Wherries sailed over the whole of Broadland to collect felled timber for such merchants as Isaac Wales, of Reedham, who numbered among his fleet the famous *Fawn.* The logs were loaded by using the winch and halyard, the latter being taken out of the herring hole and rove through a block which was chained to the mast about the level of the painted bands. The chain allowed the block to swing to the side so that the rope passing through it could point naturally in the direction of strain. The mast was half lowered and the cargo swung aboard using that stout spar as a kind of derrick.

82

On the *Olga* and *Bell,* two of Wales's wherries which were used more for timber carrying than for anything else, a sidestay was rigged for such heavy work, a tackle being made fast to a ring in the planksheer between the two forward timberheads.

Logs were loaded in the hold, and if one was too long it was usually sawn up so that it would fit. If, however, a long one was specially needed it was laid on top, overhanging the dead hatch, or else towed with other such long logs as a raft. When the raft consisted of oak logs it would sometimes sink, and the logs would have to be held up by chains made fast to the after timberheads.

These were not the only rafts seen on the rivers, for there was a time when large baulks of pitchpine were imported in Scandinavian sailing vessels, mostly barque-rigged vessels of the kind familiarly termed "onkers" because of the noise made by their windmill pumps, and brought up the river to Norwich in large rafts. The baulks were chained together into rafts perhaps as much as 300 foot long and 20 foot wide, yet one man would take charge of a raft and quant it along the river when the tide served, mooring up when it turned against him; it could take as much as a week to navigate such a raft the 27 miles up to Norwich. It appears that sometimes when the wind was just right an enterprising raftsman would even raise a makeshift sail.

Deals, sawn planks usually loaded overside from Scandinavian sailing ships or steamers in Yarmouth harbour, were loaded above the right-ups and on the plankways so that they extended two feet on either side of the hull. This produced a stack twenty feet across, giving just nine inches to spare when passing under Bishop's Bridge to reach

Account for carriage of a cargo of coal in the wherry *Macadam,* 1914.

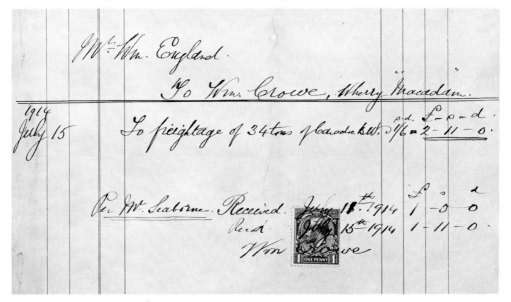

the timber yards in Colegate, in the heart of Norwich. The stack was laid fore and aft as far as the timberheads, coming right over the cabin.

Such a stack was not made in any way haphazardly. The method of loading a wherry with sawn timber was first to fill the hold to the top of the shifting right-ups, then to stack lengths of timber on the plankways about three inches higher than those in the hold; timbers were then placed across from plankway to plankway, which took the weight of the remaining part of the cargo; timbers were then again placed lengthwise to bring the load about a foot higher. In this way about 12 or 14 standards would be carried by an average wherry.

Similar cargoes included alder poles, five or six inches through, for the making of brush backs at the Wymondham brush factory. These used to be brought from the North River and unloaded at St. Ann's Staithe, in King Street, Norwich, whence they were taken to Wymondham by a great old waggon. There were also cargoes of sawn-off ends, brought from Yarmouth for making into boxwood for Cooper's, a Norwich firm of confectioners.

The Norfolk plantations provided many trawl beams for the fishing smacks of Yarmouth and Lowestoft. These were of oak, fifty to sixty feet long, made in sections scarfed together and bent to the shape of the smack's hull so that they laid comfortably along the bulwarks. Many plantations were bought by timber merchants just for this purpose, and many a cargo of beams went down to the ports.

When the dykes were laid and the upper reaches of the river were choked with ice, as they were whenever the winter was at all severe, the wherrymen turned their hands to the loading of ice cargoes. Before the end of the last century this trade was of no little importance, for the fishing fleets of Yarmouth and Lowestoft needed good supplies of ice for packing their fish, and in Norwich and other places there were icehouses where the ice was stored until it was needed later in the year.

The ice was dydled off the surface of the broads with wire dydles, which were nets about two feet across set on the ends of lengthy poles, rather similar to the implements used by the marshmen for fying out dykes. When a wherryman had a hold full of this chilly cargo he would sail down to one or other of the fishing ports and land his ice at one of the icehouses. There was one just to the southwest of the Haven Bridge at Yarmouth; this big thatched building survived for many years after the ice trade had diminished and died, finding another use as a corn store for J. & H. Bunn. Another similar thatched icehouse stood at Lowestoft, just to seaward of the swing bridge on the site now taken up by the Trawl Basin. These were not the only icehouses, for there was also one on Ice House Hill at Gorleston to which was brought ice from Norway for use by Hewett's famous Short Blue Fleet, one of the several fleets of smacks which sailed from Yarmouth for the North Sea fishing grounds in the second half of the nineteenth century. Ice was also needed by the tradesmen of Norwich before the days of refrigerators, and there was an icehouse in Ice House Lane, above King Street; this survived until 1937, though last used about 1894.

A rural icehouse was that at Surlingham. This thatched building, set on piles in the middle of the marsh, had an elevator operated by a horse gear to which the ice was floated. The ice was discharged by the elevator into metal bins in which its own weight caused it to solidify into a block. Although apparently a very up-to-date affair, it does not seem to have been a financial success and closed down after only a fairly short life. It is said that the company which owned it never paid the timber merchants for the pitchpine which went into its construction, but the merchants recovered most of the timber when the icehouse was demolished.

Ice brought by sea-going vessels from the Norwegian fjords provided competition for the Norfolk watermen. Brought in five-hundredweight blocks, this foreign product must have been rather more popular than the broadland lumps. The ice was carried ashore in baskets rather similar to those used for landing herring, and it was quite remarkable to see men sweating as they carried the baskets of ice into the icehouses.

It was not this imported ice but "artificial" ice that finally ended the Broads trade, however. When factories, first at Lowestoft and then at Yarmouth, began making ice

The curiously-shaped icehouse at Surlingham to which wherries brought ice during the winter.

about 1880 the need for natural ice declined. At first there was a prejudice against the manufactured ice, as it was said to taste of the ammonia used in the freezing plant and to taint the fish packed in it, but gradually the man-made stuff drove out its natural competitors.

It is said that in the end the ice manufacturers dealt the fresh ice trade a death blow by refusing to supply any person who took natural ice during the winter. No owner dared to buy the Broadland ice then, however much he preferred it, for fear that the natural supply would not last him through the year.

There was hardly a thing the wherries did not carry. Some of these craft even operated a service similar to that provided by the carriers' carts of the country roads, taking parcels and small quantities of goods as required. One wherry which is remembered as having taken part in this kind of trade is the *Lowestoft Trader,* whose owner sold her and replaced her by the 48-ton *Wanderer;* this big craft was not a success in such an activity, however, being too large to get alongside some of the smaller staithes.

These big wherries were mainly confined to the Norwich River and were particularly suitable for lightering cargo from ships anchored in Yarmouth Roads. In the days when the bar at the harbour mouth closed Yarmouth harbour for weeks on end to deep-draughted vessels the wherries would be employed to bring in cargo and sometimes to take coal out to steamers unable to enter harbour for bunkering.

Wherries can be seen at this work in at least two paintings by artists of the Norwich School. There is John Sell Cotman's painting in the City of Birmingham Art Gallery, which although entitled "Fishing Boats in Yarmouth Roads" shows not fishing craft but a wherry alongside a brig at anchor. Even more interesting is a picture by M. E. Cotman in the Colman Gallery of Norwich Castle Museum showing wherries unloading timber from a vessel in the roads. There is a brig at anchor with her main course backed, apparently to keep the unloading port on the starboard side clear of the water. Her other sails are furled. On the windward side is a wherry into which timber is being unloaded through the square port in the brig's side. Another wherry is under sail nearby, and what may be a wherry's sail can be seen in the distance.

With their low freeboard and comparatively flat sheer line wherries were not really very suitable craft for work at sea, yet this kind of lightering was considered all in the day's work. Though there is no known record of a wherry coming to grief while taking part in such work, there was an occasion in the winter of 1781-82 when a keel taking in coal from a collier in the Roads suddenly foundered. Ten years or so earlier another keel engaged in lightening a timber ship had been driven away and wrecked near Happisburgh.

The wherrymen received extra pay each time they went out into the Roads, and they had only to attend to their wherries, the loading being left to other men. When the tide was flowing steadily it needed only a tiller line to hold the rudder over so as to give the wherry a sheer away from the vessel's side, but it is said that when the tide was on the turn the wherries sometimes got knocked about rather heavily.

The 80-ton *Wonder,* the largest wherry built, was designed with the special object of being sent out to sea to load from ships too big to get into harbour. She carried out this part of her work satisfactorily, but it was found that she was rather too large for river work and was cumbersome in the upper reaches of the Yare above Cantley.

The owner for whom she was built, William "Dilly" Smith, sold the *Wonder* to Tom Read, the Norwich corn merchant and miller, and it was while in his ownership that she went to sea for the last time, going out from Lowestoft to get a freight of maize from a vessel anchored offshore.

That was about 1897. The last time wherries loaded at sea was on the Tuesday of August Bank Holiday week, 1898, when the *Dora, Princess* and *Wanderer* towed out of Yarmouth harbour behind a tug to take in a cargo destined for Carrow. After being loaded they went straight upriver.

It was a common practice for wherries to sail between Yarmouth and Lowestoft by sea, making the sea trip of a little over seven miles instead of the much longer inland voyage across Breydon, up the Waveney, through Oulton Dyke and over Oulton Broad, with several bridges and a lock to pass on the way.

Walter Powley, of Norwich, told of several such short trips that he made, mostly with a light wherry—if loaded he had to pay harbour dues. Once with a northerly wind he was ordered from Yarmouth to Lowestoft in company with the ironpot *Cygnus,* which was then owned by her builders, Fellows of Yarmouth; her skipper was Sam Holmes, known as "Rodney". After buying provisions they left Yarmouth together about 11 a.m. and after a short sea trip arrived in Lowestoft by 1 p.m. They loaded granite from a ship there and reached Beccles by that night.

On another occasion, when he was with Victor Welton in the *Dora* or *Maud,* he unloaded timber at Lowestoft and was then directed to Yarmouth. The light south-easterly wind would not carry the wherry out of the harbour, so they hauled round the pier and slipped slowly out on the ebb. Nearing Yarmouth they got up from the forepeak a small stocked anchor they carried for such occasions and shackled it on to the dropping chain, but a wind came up and carried them into the harbour.

Another wherryman, John Hipkin, of Trowse, has related how on one occasion he took the wherry *Herald* from Norwich to Yarmouth, where after discharging their cargo they were to proceed alongside some sea-going vessel to load up again. At Yarmouth they learnt that the vessel had put into Lowestoft, and also discovered that other wherries from Norwich that were to load from the same ship had been advised of this before leaving. If they sailed over Breydon and up by St. Olaves they would

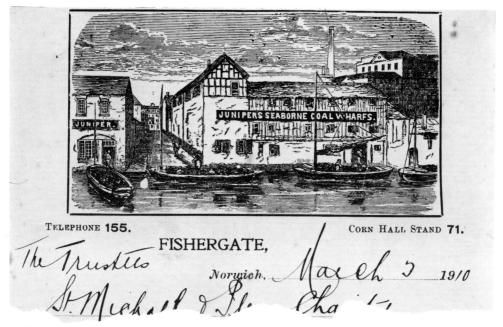

A bill heading of Robert Kerrison Juniper, a Norwich coal merchant whose premises were at the bottom of Hansard Lane (Water Lane) across the river from Quayside.

arrive after the other wherries and have to await their turn before they could receive their cargo, so they agreed to go by sea, being towed out by a tug which was taking fishing smacks out of the harbour.

The wind was from the south, which meant they had a head wind, but after three or four tacks they were abreast of Lowestoft. Just before reaching the harbour entrance the wherry was "weathercocked", as the wherryman calls it when on going about she loses way and cannot fill her sail—this sometimes happened at sea when the action of the waves on the bow hindered her in putting about. After going astern a short distance the wherry, with the help of the rudder, paid off and her sail filled. She entered harbour safely and arrived alongside the ship some minutes before the other wherries, thus getting first turn.

There was a time, too, when wherries were employed between Lowestoft and Southwold and, to judge from shipping lists in mid-nineteenth century newspapers, even in short coasting voyages on the Suffolk coast. Thaxter's *Go Forward* was for a time employed carrying bricks from Somerleyton brickworks to Southwold for some building project or other there.

The story of the *Star of Halesworth* and other wherries used on the Blyth Navigation up to Halesworth has been told in some detail elsewhere, but it is worth remembering that this Suffolk river, though separate from the Broadland river system, knew the black sails of the wherries.

Unfortunately for the wherries the Merchant Shipping Acts of 1894 and 1906 stipulated that coastwise trading vessels of over 15 tons burden must be registered and carry a certificate of registry, bills of lading, invoices containing particulars of cargo and so on which must be produced on demand. These Acts also enforced the carrying of lifesaving appliances on board and rendered the masters and owners liable to prosecution for overloading or improper loading which made craft unfit to go to sea without serious danger to life. These regulations and restrictions were the main reason for wherries ceasing to use this oversea route, which cut the time taken in sailing between Yarmouth and Lowestoft by more than half; by sea the distance could be covered in little more than an hour.

The tradition of sailing by sea from Yarmouth to Lowestoft was revived by the Wherry Trust in 1951, when the *Albion* took an hour and a half to sail from Gorleston pierhead to Lowestoft harbour, but the kind of trip which a number of wherries made almost a century earlier is never likely to be repeated.

It was in 1857 that Lucas Brothers, the Lowestoft contractors, conceived the idea of sending wherries from their Suffolk base to the Solent to solve their transport problems in connection with the building of barracks at Gosport. They inserted an advertisement in local newspapers stating that they wished to buy a number of wherries, and by March were able to send four wherries south, another four following in July. Seven reached Portsmouth, one of the first batch being lost on the way.

Among the people who were aboard the first group of wherries was a small boy, Martin Wigg, who was accompanying his father, skipper of the *Mahala*. It was he who told the story of that voyage to a correspondent of the *Eastern Daily Press* almost 70 years afterwards.

"We left Lowestoft on a Sunday morning, reached Harwich the same night, and lay in the harbour there till the following Friday morning, when we sailed from Harwich and went right through to Portsmouth," he was reported as saying. "Three of the wherries got to Portsmouth on the Saturday morning, viz"—somehow I can't imagine an old wherryman of nearly eighty saying it quite like that—"*Number One* (45 tons), *Carrow* (32 tons) and *Mahala* (24 tons). The *Accommodation* (34 tons) got into a muddle and was run ashore on the Isle of Wight. She became a total wreck."

The ill-fated *Accommodation,* it seems, lost its rudder in heavy weather and drove ashore, happily without loss of life.

Each wherry had a crew of two men, with one pilot in charge of the group from Lowestoft to Harwich and a pilot on each wherry from Harwich round to Portsmouth. The wherries carried a staysail as well as the usual big mainsail, behaving well in the strong wind and riding the seas happily enough.

As soon as the little fleet had reached Portsmouth the wherries got to work. *Number One,* being the largest of the wherries, did a lot of sea work, the smaller wherries sticking largely to the more enclosed waters. They traded to Southampton after breeze, to Langston after sea sand and over Spithead into Cowes and up the Medina to Newport for cement.

The three pioneers were joined four months later by the *Norfolk Hero Senior* (40 tons), *Wellington* (36 tons), *Dahlia* (33 tons) and *Star* (28 tons). The *Wellington* and *Star* were sent home to Lowestoft in 1858, but the *Norfolk Hero Senior* and the *Carrow* were sold to work out their remaining days in Hampshire waters.

In due course it was decided to send the three remaining wherries back to their home waters. The only call on the homeward trip was at Newhaven, for when off Harwich they encountered a strong westerly wind which prevented them getting into Harwich harbour, and they reached Lowestoft at two o'clock one morning in September, 1858.

There must have been quite a party on the *Number One* during that homeward voyage, for Wigg's father and mother, young Martin Wigg and his three-month-old sister Lizzie were all on board. The senior Wigg had transferred to command of the *Number One* while at Portsmouth.

This wherry, recorded as having been built for Lucas Brothers by Charles Reynolds of Lowestoft in 1850, finished her days in the hands of J. S. Hobrough, who used her as a dredger some three-quarters of a century after her Channel exploits.

Unloading coal from the *Volunteer* at Langley staithe. The workmen are using wheelbarrows without legs, a design peculiar to those used on wherries.

CHAPTER FIVE

Unlawful Occasions

CARGOES carried in keels and wherries were always at the mercy of dishonest watermen, and pilfering was a constant source of complaint to the merchants who depended on water transport. Whatever cargo was carried, coal, grain, malt, beer or wine, there were those who levied their toll, quite apart from the collector at Norwich.

Even when they stopped short of actual theft the criminal fringe had their ways of making "a bit on the side," as one can judge from an item among the Norwich Corporation records in 1762:

> At an assembly held the third of May, a committee appointed to enquire into the abuses committed in the measurement of coals from on board ships, and to consider of proper means to prevent such abuses for the future; the committee accordingly nominated twelve persons to be sworn as meters, who are to have 3d. per chalder for their trouble, to be paid by the buyer; and likewise drew up a set of rules and orders for their better regulation; a copy of which is to be delivered to each meter, and another hung up in the public office of the collector of the tonage duties.

All too frequently the criminal element did not stop short of wholesale robbery, however. In 1778 several merchants and owners of keels and wherries trading between Norwich and Yarmouth formed an association of the kind then popular "for the better discovering, apprehending, prosecuting and bringing to Justice all such Person or Persons who have or hath stolen, purloined or embezzled, or may at any Time or Times hereafter steal, purloin or embezzle any of their Goods, Wares, or Merchandize, belonging to any Person or Persons who are or may be Members of this Association..."

Only a lawyer could have drawn up this document, which offered a ten-guinea reward to anybody giving information "of him, her or them, who hath, or have been, or is, are or shall be guilty of the Offence or Offences aforesaid..."

Yet just twelve months after the association's inauguration the watchmen going their rounds in Conesford Street,* Norwich, saw two men coming from the river with something in a sack; the something was several cheeses which they had just stolen from a keel. And in 1781 the thieves were even operating in broad daylight; they were unloading the seventh chaldron of coal from a keel lying in the river at Norwich when they were spotted and forced to make a quick getaway.

The proprietors of the Bungay Navigation announced in 1779 that they had decided to follow the example of the Norwich merchants and had "also come to the Resolution of taking the like Measure, for the better apprehending and bringing to

*Now known as King Street.

Wherries in Yarmouth harbour. Also lying on the Southtown side of the river in this view are the little Scandinavian schooner *Marie Sophie* and a spritsail barge, while the local trawling smacks are much in evidence on the Yarmouth side.

justice all such Person or Persons as have stolen, purloined, or embezzled any Goods, Wares or Merchandize whatsoever from on board their Keels and Wherry's, or from their Warehouses or other premises ..."

Their offer to pay ten guineas for information probably had as little effect as Mr. John Sparshall's advertisement in the *Norwich Mercury* in September of the same year. Addressing his letter from North Walsham, Mr. Sparshall wrote: "Whereas I received about ten days since an anonymous letter (which was left at the *Three Horse Shoes,* at the North End, Yarmouth, directed for me) intimating that several of my Boatmen, whose names are particularly mentioned, have for some time past made a constant practice of embezzling my corn and other goods entrusted to their care, which the writer of the said letter says he can swear and bring evidence of: I do therefore in this public manner, offer the author of this letter, or any other person, a reward of 20 pounds (over and above what is allowed by Act of Parliament) if he or they will appear and prove what is therein asserted, so as the offender or offenders be convicted thereof."

The anonymous writers were busy, for a couple of years later the proprietors of the Bungay Navigation increased their offer to £20 and added: "If the Writer of an anonymous Letter directed to Mr. Cotten at Bungay, having the Beccles Post-Mark upon it, and received from thence the 10th Inst. by Post will come forth and substantially prove the Charges against the Parties therein mentioned, which he is earnestly entreated to do, he shall receive a more liberal Reward than is offered as above."

In spite of the rewards offered, the robberies went on. It was all too easy for a waterman to lay his craft alongside a quiet staithe while on his way upriver or even to lay his wherry alongside another and transfer a few sacks of coal or corn in some remote spot where the chance of detection was very small.

It should not be supposed that all watermen were rogues, however. There was, for instance, Henry Scarle of Bungay who "was valued when alive, and respected now dead," according to his gravestone in Bungay Holy Trinity churchyard. Scarle was murdered by three men he had discovered robbing his wherry and had given away to his employer, Matthias Kerrison, the Bungay merchant. The murderers attempted to escape to London but were arrested at Botesdale, thanks to the vigilance of people employed by the Bungay Association for Apprehending Felons &c.

In 1810 Norwich corn and coal merchants agreed "in consequence of the numerous depredations committed on the river between Norwich and Yarmouth not to employ any Craft, Wherry or other Vessel after the first of March next ensuing, the Hatches of which are not secured by Iron bars and locks..."

The idea was either to have two keys, one held by the agent at Yarmouth and the other by the merchant himself or to have a single key sent by coach while the wherry was on its way from Yarmouth to Norwich or vice versa. Even in 1810 the system was not new, however, for more than forty years earlier the proprietors of the Bungay Navigation had announced they were building wherries "which will be hatched, the more effectually to prevent any Fraud or Imposition by Watermen, which, after they are laden either at Bungay or Yarmouth, will be locked down, and not opened again till they arrive at the Place of Delivery."

Yet a decade after the decision by the Norwich merchants to use only locked wherries it was said that depredations on the Yare during the preceding five years had amounted to £25,000. The anonymous writers were busy in 1820, even telling the merchants in which part of the river the robberies were being perpetrated, but it was found impossible to detect the thieves because they kept too good a lookout; they could see any approaching party a long way off across the marshes.

Eventually the Norwich merchants hid men on board the wherry *Betsy* so that they could watch the thieves at their work without being noticed. The result was that more than a score of watermen and others were charged with stealing or receiving coal from various wherries.

Locks on the hatches did not save the cargo of the *Nancy* from pillage, for the watchers saw the thieves force the bar holding the hatches by hooking on the halyard and cranking away on the winch. The coal from the *Nancy* was transferred to another wherry at a quiet spot at Chedgrave known as Eight-mile Trees, but sometimes the predators were more daring. In one case they unloaded 88 skeps of coal from the *Accommodation* into a coal bin at Cantley; the master and another of the seven men involved paid for their daring with a sentence of transportation, and so did the owner of the coal bin when he was caught some months later.

These cases would never have been brought without the co-operation of the master of the *Betsy*, one William Buttle. Efforts were made at the trials to hide the identity of both Buttle and his wherry, but the story of his voyagings came out and he suffered as a result. It seems that he was employed by the city's corn and coal merchants as a "watch", a sort of river policeman, and his success in this role made him extremely unpopular with at least some of the waterside fraternity. On one occasion he was attacked with brickbats and put to flight when discovered at his work, hidden under a tarpaulin aboard a small boat.

When a committee of the House of Commons took evidence in 1826 on the Bill for making a navigation between Norwich and Lowestoft they heard a good deal about the pillage that took place on the river from Mr. Crisp Brown, who said that he exported between 900 and 1,000 quarters of corn every eight or nine days and bought three to four thousand chaldrons of coal a year at Yarmouth for resale in Norwich. These goods were, of course, carried in wherries, and the loss from transhipment and pilferage was between one and a half and two per cent. The conviction of so many men in 1820 had not ended the story of what amounted almost to piracy, for he reckoned that his loss by plunder and transhipment in the preceding year had amounted to more than £840, and within the preceding month he had found a deficiency of nearly five quarters in a cargo of 126 quarters of barley he had sent to Yarmouth. "We cannot detect the thieves now," he added, "they keep so good a lookout."

Some were careless, though, for in 1830 thieves who were helping themselves to a sample of malt from the hold of a wherry moored at Coldham Hall were caught in the act by representatives of the owner who had rowed downriver in a boat. The result was that the master of the wherry was sentenced to transportation for no less a period than fourteen years.

Two other men, one a wherryman and the other the landlord of a public house at Coldham Hall, received similar sentences about the same time for stealing nine gallons of port wine from the cargo of a wherry. The hoops of the pipes of wine were driven back, spile-holes were made, and about three gallons of wine taken out of each pipe. The pipes were then topped up with water, the holes stopped up and the hoops

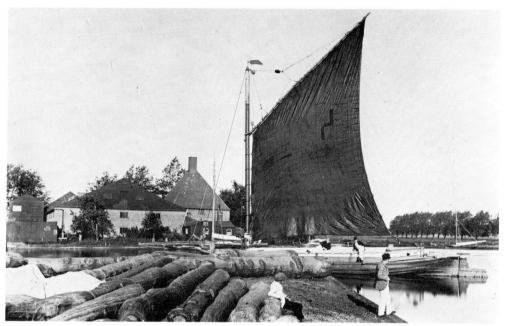

Beccles staithe in the days when it was reckoned that the best oak timber came from the Beccles area. The wherry has its winch fitted to the tabernacle.

driven back, and had they not been given away by an accomplice the thieves would probably have remained undiscovered, though the wine-merchant's customers would undoubtedly have complained of the quality of the port.

Arthur Patterson, in his fine book *Wildfowlers and Poachers,* tells the story of a rather similar crime perpetrated by a member of the Breydon fraternity. Boarding a wherry one day and using a gimlet to draw beer from one of the barrels that formed the cargo, he found he had no receptacle for his stolen liquor; so he filled his two muddy old patched water-boots brimful of beer.

It seems strange that such large-scale plunder could go on virtually unchecked for so long, but the Broads were not then the holiday resort of thousands that they are today. Those who lived and had their business on the rivers and among the reed beds of this region led a lonely life.

Some of those who lived at lonely spots were not above doing a spot of "shaving," helping to dispose of the odd sack or two of coal or grain which a wherryman might help himself to while on his way up or down river. It is said that the *Cockatrice,* a long-defunct hostelry on the Yare, standing on the road from Heckingham to Reedham

Stacks of bricks on the North Quay at Yarmouth are evidence of a flourishing trade; wherrymen were careful to ensure that some of their cargoes were less exposed to public gaze.

Ferry, was well placed for this illicit trade as it was off the Reedham policeman's beat and warning of the Loddon bobby's approach could always be gained in time.

On one occasion, if the tale told by old Tom George, of the *Acle Bridge Hotel,* be true, the policeman actually lent a hand to unload some stolen cargo from a wherry. The story goes that the landlord was expecting some sacks of grain, but knowing the policeman was on the prowl he locked up the inn and retired to bed early. On arriving at the staithe the wherryman made such noisy and persistent efforts to waken the landlord that the policeman eventually came out of his hiding place to see what was going on. The wherryman spun him a yarn that he'd been ordered to unload part of his cargo there and he was anxious to get help as otherwise he'd lose his tide. He expressed his opinion of the landlord, on whom he said he had relied for assistance, in no uncertain manner and made his tale sound so convincing that in the end the unsuspecting policeman volunteered to help him unload.

Like those caught by the "watch" in 1820, however, the culprits did not always escape detection. In 1855 five watermen and a labourer were brought before the magistrates at Bungay and charged with stealing coal from the wherry *Gem,* which had been lying at the staithe. It was said the men had transferred the coal from the *Gem* to another wherry lying some sixty yards down the dyke.

Less than three years later two watermen, the master of the wherry *Albert* and his son, were charged at Bungay with stealing barley belonging to Mr. David Walker, the Bungay maltster. Two sacks of the barley, which had been consigned to a firm at Newark and was to be transhipped from the wherry to a seagoing vessel at Crisp's Wharf, Beccles, were found in the wherryman's bunk after there had been a complaint of a shortage in the amount transhipped.

A wherryman who in 1859 was sent to prison for nine months for stealing part of his cargo of Blyth steam coals seems to have used tactics similar to those which must have been employed by the pillagers who so worried Mr. Crisp Brown years before. He took in fifteen tons of coal at Yarmouth, but delivered only fourteen tons at the Burgh Castle cement works, to which many a wherry load of coal was consigned. Being ordered to proceed to Norwich for a freight of stones, he landed two sacks at Reedham, sold a tumbler load to a publican at Thorpe, and passed a further eight sacks to another receiver.

The *Norwich Mercury's* comment on this case makes it clear that even at this date it was no isolated instance of dishonesty. "From the statement of the prisoner and another wherryman, and a boy, it was proved that a most extensive system of plunder is carried on by the wherrymen employed in carrying coals, and all persons who are interested in the trade would do well to ascertain on delivery the quantity they actually receive," the newspaper advised.

It was not only coal that disappeared in transit, for in 1865 the master of the wherry *Eclipse* was charged with the theft of two or three tons of pig iron, part of a consignment of about eighty tons sent from Yarmouth for a Norwich foundry.

Oulton Broad.

Not all wherrymen were rogues, however, for when two Beccles wherrymen were charged with stealing six stones of oil cake in 1870 the Lowestoft Magistrates dismissed the case. From the evidence they heard it appeared that the cake had slipped down among some sacks of maize which were also in the cargo of the wherry *Emmet*.

Smuggling as well as plunder was a paying occupation for the master of a wherry, and many must be the cargo that has been carried quietly along the rivers unknown to the Customs men. Tradition has it that many a windpump and riverside barn served as a cache for smuggled goods. And Broadland folklore tells of the windmill sails being used to signal messages across the marshes, sometimes giving warning of the movements of the Revenue men.

One hears only of the unsuccessful runs, as in 1850 when a large seizure of contraband tobacco was made at Yarmouth. Nearly 6,500lb. of superior leaf tobacco was found on board a wherry, into which it had just been loaded from a small Cromer fishing boat.

More than twenty years earlier the local newspapers had recorded the capture of a 39-foot "smuggling galley" on Breydon. When the Yarmouth tide surveyor, Mr. Brightin Silvers, made the capture after a five-mile chase the crew of nine made good their escape across the marshes, but they left behind 283 half-ankers of proof brandy and about 6,000 lb. of tobacco.

Usually, though, the cargoes that were landed on dark nights on the deserted beaches to the north of Yarmouth were quietly carried by cart across the marshes and as quietly loaded into a waiting wherry. Perhaps a stack of marsh hay or reeds or a few sacks of corn hid the contraband; none knew of the wherry's hidden cargo save the smugglers and their accomplices, and they "weren't sayin' nuth'n." A few captures were made, such as when a reed barge with a contraband cargo was seized on Hickling Broad, but of the successful runs it was a case of "don't you know nothin', they can't get over that," and they have gone unrecorded.

Generally there was none of the drama of the long, hard chase. A veteran wherry-man, William Royall, who died in 1936 at the ripe old age of 83, used to tell how his grandfather had once carried a cargo of contraband goods which had been landed on the denes at Caister and taken in carts across the marshes, probably down some little-frequented track that led to a farmhouse near the river Bure. His grandfather sailed the wherry to Thorpe St. Andrew to unload the cargo of spirits, silk or whatever it was, not daring to bring it right into Norwich. Unfortunately for him the Revenue men got wind of what was afoot and on the green near the old church at Thorpe the wherryman and the recipients of the cargo were all arrested.

Grandfather Royall went to prison and cargo and wherry were confiscated. But, according to the story, the wherry was commandeered by some friends of the family who sailed it to Oulton Broad and sank it there. When the sentence was completed the wherry was retrieved, the water pumped out and Royall resumed his interrupted wherry trading.

It must be remembered that at that time there was no Cut and no railway bridge at Thorpe, and all craft going up to Norwich passed the village green.

There were other illegal games for which wherries came in handy, too. Cock-fighting was outlawed in 1835, but the "sport" enjoyed a considerable following even after Parliament had voted to make it illegal and there were still many good sportsmen who subscribed to the ditty

> To keep game cocks and hunt the fox,
>   To drink the punch and whisky,
> We fear no locks, we'll train the cocks
>   And care not if it's risky.

Many a main of cocks was arranged in barns on farms near the river, transport for the birds and their supporters being arranged by wherry.

Large numbers of "the fancy" also used to take to the water to reach the scene of those illegal meetings known in the last century as "pugilistic encounters," wherries being convenient vessels for reaching the most isolated spots where the likelihood of interference by the minions of the law was least. One favourite spot was Burgh Castle, because if the Suffolk police intervened the crowd was able to cross over to the Norfolk side of the river. There were always wherries lying at the cement works that could be used to carry a large number of people across to the marshes on the opposite bank if necessary, and as this was a particularly inaccessible spot they were not likely to be interfered with again.

It is said that sometimes the "Peelers" showed considerable ingenuity and determination in reaching the scene of an encounter in order to break up the illegal gathering. A Yarmouth wherryman, Jack Thompson, was nearing his century when in 1931 he told the story of an incident perhaps seventy years earlier when the police found boats in which to cross the river to the marsh on which a fight was in progress. The oars had been carefully removed; but, nothing daunted, the policemen used their top hats to paddle themselves across.

Sometimes the wherries were thought hardly fine enough for the gentlemen of the ring and chartered steam vessels were used to carry them to the chosen place, as in 1857 when two such encounters took place on the south-west bank of the Yare about a mile and a half above Berney Arms. On this occasion the steam tug *Post Boy* was chartered from Norwich for the excursion.

In days when municipal elections at Norwich rivalled Eatanswill in their corruption and it was stated that "bribery at Norwich is as common as the sun at noonday," wherries were called into requisition for yet another purpose, namely "cooping." This was a means of ensuring that the "right party" got the most votes, or rather of ensuring that the rival party did not get the votes of all its supporters, who were seized and put on board wherries until the election was over.

The process is well described in a report published just before the passing of the Municipal Corporations Act of 1835: "It consists sometimes in seizing and confining the voters of the opposite party during the time of an election, and keeping them in confinement till the poll is closed, or till they are induced to promise their votes to the party confining them. On other occasions voters have been cooped by their own friends to prevent violence or seduction by the opposing party.

"This practice has frequently been resorted to by both parties. There is no doubt that it is sometimes done with the consent of the persons cooped, but proof was adduced before us of cases attended with circumstances of great brutality, in which the persons confined were taken by force and detained against their will."

The Commissioners who drew up the report had heard plenty of evidence of how supporters of one candidate had been kidnapped in broad daylight by ruffians in the pay of the other party and had been taken to Panxworth *Lion,* where they were confined to a room for a day and a night. Then they were taken by coach to Ranworth, the sober inside the coach, the drunken ones outside; with guards armed with pokers and sticks to make sure they did not escape. At Ranworth they were put on board a wherry which was moored in the middle of the broad.

One man tried to escape by boat, but was recaptured, and then a rescue attempt was made by a wherry whose skipper was in the pay of the other party. This attempt failed because the "guards" threatened to use the scythes they carried to cut down anybody who boarded, but it was enough to persuade those in charge to take the wherry-load of would-be voters off to Horsey Mere for even safer keeping.

The prisoners seem to have been well fed, and many of them were certainly drunk. The man in charge said he "did not measure out the beer, for that was too tiresome, and I served them wholesale." And, truth to tell, it seems as if getting them drunk and keeping them drunk, and even giving them drugs, was a way of ensuring that they did not escape. One man who did keep both sober and alert managed to jump ashore as the wherry made its way up the Thurne, but it was five days before the rest were returned to their homes.

What lawless days those were in Britain.

CHAPTER SIX

The Watermen

WHAT KIND of men were they who sailed the keels and wherries from Yarmouth to Norwich and all round the Norfolk and Suffolk waterways? Were they really a race apart, as has been suggested by some writers?

The Norfolk waterman was no superior being, no resident of Olympus come down to Earth, but like all watermen of the old school he knew his craft and the waters in which he spent his life, and he was remarkably skilled at getting the best out of his craft in all conditions.

He sailed all the year round, or at least he kept sailing until the rivers froze up and prevented his wherry from working on. Then, perhaps, he would look to icing to turn an opportune honest penny. And in so doing he learnt many a trick; no spare-time, fine weather sailor he.

It is interesting to note that quite a number of watermen were freemen of Norwich and Yarmouth at a time when the freedom was a valuable appurtenance, giving the holder the right to vote at elections. According to a list of freemen of Yarmouth from 1429 to 1800 the first keelman, Robert Hall, was admitted to the freedom in 1502 and the last keelman to appear in the list was admitted in 1795; the first wherryman, Matthew Underwood, had been admitted twelve years earlier.

Early accounts of both keels and wherries tell us that the watermen frequently carried their families with them as they sailed the rivers, and it was by no means unknown for the mate of a wherry and the wherryman's wife to be one and the same. "These vessels are seldom navigated by more than two hands, and one of them is often a boy, or the wife of the waterman; in the latter case it is not infrequent for them to have their families in a cabin placed at the stern," observed the author of *A Norfolk Tour* in 1829.

The wherryman's wife can be seen at the tiller in a water colour of the river near King Street, Norwich, painted by John Thirtle in 1817 and now in the Castle Museum, Norwich. The wherryman himself is quanting his wherry downriver.

In later days, however, it was usual for the family to have a little cottage in one of the marsh villages or in one of the towns in which the family could live while father was sailing the waterways to earn a living. George Applegate, who lived to be over ninety and the oldest inhabitant of Potter Heigham, married in 1850 at the age of twenty-five and for the first three years of their married life he and his young wife lived on board the wherry he owned. When, with the arrival of a family, they settled in

Potter Heigham he worked the wherry single-handed most of the time in order to save the expense of employing a mate.

He worked the same wherry for many years, until one morning he awoke to find his shoes floating about in the cabin, and the wherry settling down in the water.

How some of these old-time wherrymen managed to bring up quite large families in such cramped quarters as were provided by the cabin of a wherry is beyond comprehension. Some of the older children no doubt had to sleep in the forepeak, but even so it must have been a dreadfully overcrowded existence they led.

Not only was it an overcrowded life but a pretty primitive one to boot. The stoves fitted in the cabins of the older wherries were small, not much more than a foot wide, allowing space for lockers between the stove and the bunks which ran along each side of the cabin. On these stoves it was possible to do no more than boiling and frying, so it is not surprising that larger stoves incorporating a small oven were installed in later craft.

These stoves gave out much more heat than the old ones, and the wooden chimneys which were a feature of the wherry often became scorched. Because of this the wooden chimneys were gradually discarded in favour of iron stovepipes with a hood on top.

In summer the larger stoves made the tiny cabins unbearably hot, so many wherries had a small basket-shaped brazier with an iron plate placed across the top on which the wherryman's wife could do her cooking. These braziers were generally to be found on the foredeck. Besides keeping the cabin cool this arrangement had the added advantage that all smell of burnt fat and cooking was kept from hanging about the cabin, but again nothing more than frying and boiling could be done on this kind of fire.

When in Yarmouth harbour the early nineteenth century wherryman suffered from the same handicap as the seaman who sailed on deep water; because of the danger of serious fires a harbour regulation forbade the use of any lights or fires on vessels moored at the quays. Whereas at some ports such as Ipswich licences could be obtained from the harbour master permitting fires to be lighted, at Yarmouth the prohibition was absolute, and cooking had to be done in sheds erected on the quay.

In 1843 John Trunch of the wherry *Industry* and the master of a fishing smack were fined for having lights on their vessels at night, "which will be a caution to others in their situation." These regulations, imposed by an Act passed in 1771, were relaxed when steamships came into use.

Some idea of the dangers that young families faced when afloat can be gained from an incident which occurred in 1886. Two boys were drowned after falling from a wherry moored at Brundall while on its way from Yarmouth to Norwich with coal for the Norwich Gas Company. Evidence at the inquest showed that the wherryman

William Royall on his wherry, the *Spray*. He was 80 when this photograph was taken in March 1933.

had with him not only the woman with whom he had been living for twenty years (they had, it seems, never troubled to obtain the Church's blessing on their union) but his three sons, one a child in arms. It seems little wonder that in such conditions as must have existed in the wherry's tiny cabin five of their nine children had died in infancy; it is little more surprising that one had been drowned out of a mussel boat at Yarmouth and that the other two had been lost while fishing from the deck of their father's wherry.

Many a wherryman's son lived to make old bones, however. Samuel Lodge, one of the latter-day wherrymen, used to say that he wasn't born on a wherry but that at least he was bred in one. He was apprenticed to become a printer, but "I had water on the brain and I had to go back to it. You see, my father was a wherryman and although we had a good home in Yarmouth my mother and I were nearly always on the wherry. I used to attend school at Yarmouth for two or three days and then came to school in Norwich for a few days."

That was in the second half of the nineteenth century. Earlier there had been no kind of schooling at all for such youngsters, and all they knew was life on board a wherry; all they learnt was how to sail, how to work the tides, how to fish and, some said, how to steal. It has been pointed out in an earlier chapter that the morals of many wherrymen were not above reproach, and it was complained in 1820 when plunder was rife that "by the present mode of conveying property, the wherries are under the care of one family, and thus the wife and son become witnesses and participators of the crime, and we have repeated instances of young men regularly and systematically trained up in this species of pillage."

Though some of them, like poor Henry Scarle of Bungay, were shining examples of loyalty to their employers, the watermen seem generally to have been looked on with suspicion, and the worst was invariably thought of them. Perhaps it was felt because of their pitifully low wages they must resort to crime in order to live; certainly there were some who gave the impression that they believed the only honest wherryman was a dead 'un.

There were, of course, some who saw in such poor conditions an opportunity for evangelism and the winning of souls as well as a necessity for improvement, and so it was that in 1858 the Norfolk and Suffolk Wherrymen's Mission came into being. It had its beginnings in a building on Yarmouth's North Quay and fairly soon expanded into further premises, including a New Mission at Yarmouth which had formerly been the *Globe* public house, "notorious for the peculiar infamy and variety of the sins which found a congenial theatre there." Once the Devil had been given notice to quit this building was used for a Sunday School, Ragged School and Mission services, the Old Mission on North Quay being retained for Sunday School classes and meetings.

There was also a Wherrymen's and Workingmen's Institute on North Quay and a mission boat working up the rivers and down the harbour about three times a week.

In 1859 the Mayor of Yarmouth laid the foundation stone of St. Andrew's, to be known for over a century as the Wherrymen's Church, and the building was consecrated the following autumn. Those responsible for its design had the happy idea of covering the capitals of the pillars with carvings of water plants. The building was designed to hold 404 people, but it regularly held congregations of half as many again, while on summer Sunday afternoons open-air preachings were held on board wherries moored alongside the quay.

This was only part of the mission's work. In 1861, for instance, well over 5,000 visits were made to houses in the poorer parts of Yarmouth and more than 3,000 visits were made to wherries, while branches of the mission operated at Norwich and Aylsham. At the latter place a chapel was built for the wherrymen's use.

The mission was well supported for a time by philanthropists from all over the country, while annual subscribers included the Aylsham Navigation Company and a number of wherry owners.

The wherrymen might not be a separate race, but certainly the nature of their work set them apart to some extent from those who worked on the farms. Some were indeed seamen and fishermen who had decided to find a relatively easier life on the inland waterways, others were men who had never been to sea except to sail out into Yarmouth Roads or along the coast as far as Southwold; but all knew how to handle their craft superbly well.

Living their lives on the rivers, dependent on the wind and the tide, the watermen learnt how to predict the weather for hours ahead with an accuracy not surpassed by the sophisticated weathermen of the Meteorological Office today. A yachtsman who sailed the Broads nearly half a century ago has told me of passing a wherry moored near Whiteslea Lodge, the headquarters of the bird sanctuary at the entrance to Hickling Broad, as he sailed from the Hickling *Pleasure Boat Inn* on his way to Horsey Mere. The wherryman inquired where he was bound, and on being told remarked that the yachtsman would have a favourable wind, and that directly he got to the Mere the wind would spring up from the opposite direction to give him a fair wind for the return journey. It happened just as the wherryman had forecast. Surely a remarkable example of weather observation and prediction, though some superstitious people might have accused the wherryman of being a wizard and causing the weather to do what he wanted; he was waiting for the wind to change so it would be favourable for him across Hickling Broad and up Catfield Dyke.

The same yachtsman's first contact with a wherryman was when as a small boy he used to be invited for sails in a yacht skippered by a former wherryman. Whenever this

Salvaging the wherry *Express* after she had sunk with a cargo of deals.

skipper saw any erratic sailing he would say "Some Robinsons ahead, sir." He was sure that Robinson Crusoe did not know how to sail, otherwise he would never have been shipwrecked, so anyone who could not sail he called Robinson.

Perhaps their sense of humour was basically that of the ordinary Norfolk man, but it had a tang of the sea with it. Wherrymen's tales were often little more than crude fabrications or near-fabrications about the doings of some of their fraternity they considered "not quite all there." For example, there was the story of the wherryman whose numbed fingers let slip the kettle he was filling from the river; quick as thought he whipped out his shut-knife and cut a snotch in the planksheer of the wherry so's he'd know where he'd dropped the kettle when he next came that way.

Then there was the tale of a certain wherryman who, every night before turning in, used to bait a line, hoping by morning to have caught an eel for his breakfast. Even when he became skipper of a yacht he carried on his customary ritual. One Acle regatta after he had retired to his bunk other skippers hauled in his line, baited it with a weighted rabbit and cast it back into the river. Next morning when he pulled in his line and discovered the rabbit he was heard to mutter, "I're heard of a rabbit swimmin' 'cross a stream, but I nivver knew afore that rabbits'd run along the bottom of a river."

With the popularising of the Broads as a holiday resort the wherrymen could turn their scorn to the holidaymakers. There's the story they used to tell about a fellow in a motor cruiser which was in collision with a sailing yacht. The hole made in the cruiser's side by the yacht's bowsprit was well above the waterline, but this fellow decided it was imperative to get the damage repaired as soon as possible for fear the cruiser should founder when the tide rose.

Some were not above making capital out of the holiday parties, though sometimes advertisers of wherries and yachts for hire took pains to mention that the skippers and stewards were of impeccable character. The less scrupulous skippers of pleasure wherries found it paid them to get their wives to send them a telegram wishing them many happy returns of the day. Week after week the skipper got a similar telegram, which was invariably shown to the hirers, who had probably seen it delivered anyway, and of course they had a whip round for him or else stood him numerous drinks at the inn. It was not entirely for the sake of the hirers that pleasure wherry skippers contended that all the best moorings were those alongside public houses.

The skippers found that the results of the trick more than compensated them for the cost of the telegram, but of course care was needed if the same party chartered the wherry the following year for a different week.

Those who sailed the keels and wherries certainly did know how to handle their craft, yet in spite of their proficiency accidents did happen from time to time. Many a

Raising the *Lowestoft Trader* at Berney Arms in May, 1910. A platform has been built from the former steam wherry *Wensum* over the sunken craft and chains have been passed beneath the hull.

Salvaging the *Fir* after she had been sunk in collision with the steamer *Norwich Trader* at Claxton in June, 1930. In this case a platform has been built between the *John Henry*, the nearest wherry, and another wherry in order to raise the casualty.

waterman died as a result of falling overboard; it is an odd thing that a great many who found their livelihood on the water never learned to swim.

In 1779, for instance, John Aggs fell overboard from his keel when a rope he was hauling broke, and although would-be rescuers were soon on the scene he lost his life. Another waterman was lost when quanting a wherry near Whitefriars Bridge, Norwich, in 1838, and there were numerous similar cases.

The dangers were magnified when a man was sailing alone. In 1898 Wallace Solomon, a wherryman from Carlton Colville, was drowned between Somerleyton and Oulton Broad when, it was supposed, he fell from the wherry *Reedbird,* which he was working single-handed.

Stress of weather, collisions and groundings took their toll. One might have expected the risk of shipwreck to be slight enough on such inland waters, but the risk was there all the same. In 1770, for instance, "the violence of the current drove two keels on shore in Surlingham Meadows" and in the same year a keel laden with London goods sprang a leak and sank in the river at Norwich.

A rather similar accident occurred at Norwich in 1805 as a result of a combination of circumstances thus described in local newspapers: "During the violence of the gale on Sunday night a keel laden with goods, lying near a wharf in King-street, was sunk. The accident is thus accounted for. The vessel was aground on the side next the shore, and during the night the works of the New Mills being stopped, occasioned the water to fall considerably, which caused the keel to lean very much, when a gust of wind threw her upon her side."

Gale damage was more often simpler in nature, as in 1836 when a large wherry loaded with tallow, porter, sugar, salt and other goods for Norwich was swamped as she crossed Breydon in a severe storm which whipped the river into a sheet of foam.

An inscription on a headstone in Thurlton churchyard records an accident which occurred in 1809. "Sacred to the memory of Joseph Bexfield who was unfortunately drowned on the 11th of August 1809 in ye 38th Year of his Age leaving a disconsolate Widow and two Children to deplore his loss." The wherry portrayed on the headstone provides a clue, but one has to turn to the local newspapers of the day to discover exactly what did happen on that sad occasion.

> A very lamentable accident happened at Reedham . . . It is the custom to get up the meadow hay there in wherries and other craft, and when the workmen are late, it frequently occurs that they sleep on board. Five men and a boy were sleeping upon the hay in one of these vessels when, about eleven o'clock at night, during the very heavy storm of thunder and lightning, the hay gave way, from some unknown cause, and the people were precipitated into the river, where four of the men found their death.

There was no State insurance scheme in those days, and sad indeed was the position of the woman who was widowed by such an accident. The owner whose wherry was sunk or damaged in collision might also find himself in dire straits as a result of such an accident.

The Friendly Societies were an attempt to fill the needs of the working men by giving them relief in time of sickness and by supporting their dependants after the loss of the breadwinner, while shipowners' mutual insurance associations formed in many of the country's seaports enabled the owners to cover themselves against financial loss. It is impossible to say how many wherrymen were members of Foresters' courts and Odd Fellows' lodges, but in 1880 a number of owners got together to form the Wherry Owners' Insurance Friendly Society for their mutual benefit.

The Society was, according to its printed rules, established for the relief of members in case of loss by sinking or stranding of wherries. The protection was limited to expenses connected with raising and floating wherries sunk through collision or other cause or to launching and floating wherries that might get ashore out of the regular channel, and to the conveyance of the cargo on board a wherry in such trouble.

The premium was only five shillings a year for each wherry until 1921, when it jumped to £1, but claims in the event of sinking or stranding were limited to £20, possibly rising to £25 when the premium was increased. The cost of raising a sunken wherry was only £8 0s. 8d. in 1881, and never more than £10 until 1900. Up to that time it would seem that salvage operations had been carried out by members called upon by the committee to do so; the rules were that "members of this society and the masters of entered wherries in their employ shall assist in raising or launching any wherry insured in the society when required by the committee." After the turn of the century some of the operations seem to have necessitated more professional services, mainly if not solely provided by the firm of James Hobrough & Son.

One of the casualties which came under the Society's aegis was Walter Bunn's *Bell*, which was sunk at the west end of Breydon in 1906. She was towing upriver behind a Dutch steamer when the towing vessel grounded near the "Dickey Works" at the entrance to the Yare. The steamer quickly went astern to get herself off the mud and the *Bell*, laden with 40 tons of stone taken from the steamer to lighten her, ran up under her stern, the steamer's screw knocking a hole in the wherry's bow. She sank at once in 10 foot of water, the two men on board having a narrow escape. The "club" paid out the maximum £20 to have her raised, plus £3 5s. for "labor." Was this a way of getting round the £20 maximum, one wonders.

An earlier incident in the same area concerned the *Five Brothers,* whose sail was blown to pieces when crossing Breydon in a strong gale in 1894. She was blown right across the flats and ended up against the south wall. A channel had to be cut to get her back to deep water; surprisingly, this was done for as little as £6 12s. She seems not to have been the only wherry to find herself in such a predicament, for ten years previously the Society had paid £2 5s. for "Taking Cargo out of *Two Sisters* and Launching her off Ground on Breydon."

In 1908 there were sixty-seven wherries on the Society's books, but six years later there were only fifty-six. By the end of the 1914-18 war there were no more than thirty-five, and in spite of a rally in 1920 the decline continued. By 1929 the number was down to sixteen, more than half of them belonging to J. S. Hobrough, and the following year there were only seven. It was then decided that as more comprehensive means of cover were obtainable from other sources and as wherries were being displaced by other and larger craft the society should be dissolved.

Accidents still happened, though. On January 21, 1929, the *Plane,* formerly the *Albion* and renamed when the Great Yarmouth Shipping Company bought her from Watney Combe Reid & Co. Ltd., was dropping through the Haven Bridge at Yarmouth when she hit part of the structure. The old bridge was then being replaced by the present double lifting bridge, and piling put in during this operation was proving a hazard to small craft. She sank on the east side of the river near the General Steam Navigation Company's berth, where she was to have unloaded into one of the company's steamers.

While she was held up by chains made fast to the quay on one side and to a lighter on the other, the wherry was unloaded by a crane stepped in the lighter *Silver Birch*.

As a result of the accident the Great Yarmouth Port and Haven Commissioners decided that while the west pier of the old Haven Bridge was being demolished all sailing craft should be required to take tug assistance, and Hobrough's steam tug *Weasel* was hired. In little more than a week she assisted thirteen wherries and four lighters through the bridge.

The *Albion* was in trouble more than twenty years later, after being taken over by the Norfolk Wherry Trust and given back her old name. She was again salvaged and was refitted and kept in service by the Trust, a splendid anachronism, to show modern man a glimpse of a way of life that has gone for ever. But for most of her sisters such an event was the end.

Four wherries provided the flotation for this pontoon bridge erected across the Yare at Whitlingham on the occasion of a fete given by the Mayor of Norwich, Mr. Russell Colman, in 1902 to celebrate the Coronation of Edward VII. For the convenience of craft navigating the river a section of the bridge could be moved by means of winches and chains.

CHAPTER SEVEN

The Wherry Builders

THE SHORES of the broads and the banks of the Norfolk and Suffolk rivers supported many a small building yard in which wherries and smaller craft were turned out. Some produced many superb wherries—Allen's yard at Coltishall, the yards owned by the Hall family of Reedham, the Wrights of Beccles and others spring to mind—while others produced only one or two wherries among the many reed barges and marshmen's punts that they built.

The weatherboarded and red-tiled sheds of the old yards were scenes of great activity in the old days. The gnarled limbs of venerable oak trees were shaped with the adze into ribs and knees, while in the sawpit the two sawyers, one above, one below, cut whole trees of oak or elm lengthwise into strakes. There was usually a pile of twisted timber lying around, for the shape of a piece of wood dictated its use; if a knee was required, a piece was selected that could be used with the least of trimming with axe and adze.

The timber was mostly locally grown. The old builders bought trees as they lay in the wood and had them carted to the building yards, where they set to work to cut them up on the sawpit. Mr Geoffrey ffiske, who died while this book was being written, recalled travelling round the Hoveton Estate with Ernest Collins, the Wroxham boat and wherry builder, in his pony trap when the latter was choosing oak trees for the building of the little pleasure wherry *Liberty*; he was impressed by the fact that Collins often ignored those with good trunks and usually chose trees whose branches showed plenty of grown crooks suitable for cutting into curved timbers and knees. Possessing much knowledge of different kinds of locally grown wood and of their fitness for ribs, planks, floor timbers, knees and brackets, the builders scoured the woodlands of Norfolk and Suffolk for their requirements.

They generally found material near at hand. In the 1880s the plantations in the neighbourhood of Aylsham, Cawston, Itteringham, Lenwade and Attlebridge, with their many towering trees, were the principal places for supplying wherry builders. Felthorpe and Taverham and Costessey woods and plantations supplied the wherry builders and the shipbuilders of Yarmouth, and also provided trawl beams for the fishing smacks, while wherry builders at Sutton used to get their timber from Gunton Park. Some declared, however, that the best timber of all came from the Beccles district.

Larch for the masts of wherries (before being superseded by imported pitchpine) came from Costessey Park.

T. F. Goodall wrote in 1886 of the attraction of these Norfolk boatyards, but already the scene was changing and the days of many of these picturesque old yards were numbered. "A ponderous square horse-ferryboat will, perhaps, be hauled up for its periodical dressing. Boats of all kinds lie around, with various ailments—some past cure, others waiting their turn for treatment by the busy boat-doctor.

"There, too, are the battered rusty jacks made by the old boat-wright's grandfather, and the weather-beaten windlass which, pulling on the huge purchase-blocks, has for a century past drawn the great wherries, slowly but surely, high and dry from the water.

"By the saw-pit lies a pile of tough oak, whole trunks or twisted limbs, which will be cut and fashioned into timbers or stout knees for the wherries. A well-worn grindstone stands close to the vine-covered wall of the workshop; the windows are

A wherry under construction in a yard at Carrow in the early nineteenth century.

glazed with knobbly lumps of glass in a leaden setting; the ancient doors and shutters, used ever since they were hung to try the colours and clean the brushes of the painters, are ponderous with accumulated paint and gaudy with every hue of crude colour. Inside is the time and work-worn bench, the big wooden vice, rows of long augers, and tools of every description."

For the old builders their eye was their guide. When some of the old fellows looked at a plank they would know just what it would make without much measuring. Many of them could make the first strake by eye, and then carry on making the following strakes without ever measuring up, depending almost entirely on the eye. Generally they were not far out, though occasionally a particular wherry was reputed to be "wrung".

As with all clinker-built craft, the shell of a wherry was erected first and the framing put in only when the planking was complete. Some builders seem to have used but a single mould in order to produce a good section, but at Allen's at Coltishall three half-moulds of half-inch wood were employed.

When putting on the strakes the builders heated them in order to make them pliable. Whereas many a boatbuilder and shipbuilder used a steam chest for this purpose the wherry builder had a more primitive way of achieving the same object, using small bunches of reed set alight and held to the boards; the job had to be done carefully so that the boards were warmed through but not burned or damaged in any way.

The form of a wherry varied much with the builder as well as with the period of its building. Each builder had his own peculiarity; wherries built by John Allen, for instance, had straighter sides than those built by other craftsmen, and there can be no doubt that there was something about certain of the wherries built by the Hall family at Reedham that made them the fastest afloat.

To Allen's fell the honour of building the last trading wherry, the *Ella,* launched in the year of the great flood, 1912, and still afloat as a trader half a century later. The scholarly named *Primus* and *Secunda,* the latter known along the waterside as the *Blood-and-Thunder,* were other products of this yard, which was still turning out yachts and motor cruisers long after the wherries had ceased to pay. The beams of their old shed must have been like a history book, for it is said that the name of every vessel built there, and the date of its launching, was chalked on them.

Allen's was not the only yard turning out wherries at Coltishall in the nineteenth century, nor was Coltishall the only place in the upper reaches of the Bure to see the birth of these craft. In the 1840s and 1850s Thomas Wright was building wherries at Coltishall, and Elijah Wright built the famous *Gipsy,* destined to sail to foreign parts under the ownership of H. M. Doughty, at Aylsham in 1875.

At Barton Staithe the Cox family, who carried on building marshmen's boats and punts for many a year, once produced bigger craft. The last wherry they built was the 20-ton *Ethnie,* which was launched in 1894. Intended for owners on the North Walsham and Dilham Canal, she had a beam of 12 foot 4 inches, the maximum for a wherry trading above Wayford Bridge; she later became the property of Pallett, Barclay & Co. of North Walsham.

Allen's yard at Coltishall, with three wherries hauled out in the open and another in the boarded and pantiled boatshed. Two of the wherries in the open have transom sterns.

A wherry hauled out in a curious open-sided shed at Ludham, possibly Robert Harrison's yard.

Quite a few wherries were built by the Southgate family and at least one other builder at Sutton, at the head of Sutton Broad to the east of the River Ant just above Barton Broad. As many as three wherries were built in a single year by the older Southgate, no mean feat when one considers the methods then used for cutting out the timber for a wherry; Southgate never had more than five or six men working for him, so all must have been kept hard at work that year.

After many years of building at Sutton Richard Southgate took stock of his affairs and found that he was just a pound on the right side. Prospects were not rosy, and he decided to emigrate to America, but when Thomas Worts, of Sutton Mill, heard this he gave Southgate the job of building the wherry *Kearsage,* which in later years was the last to trade up to Sutton. The last wherry built at Sutton was the *Margaret,* built for Hudson Barber in 1887 by Ted Southgate, one of Richard Southgate's two sons. A little later the family did move, but only as far as Stalham, where Ted (known as "Nelson" because he had lost the sight of one eye), and his brother George set up as boat builders and hirers.

One of the Southgates' employees was Josiah Cubitt Teasel, who after leaving their employ built three or four wherries on his own account at Stalham. One of his wherries was the *Ceres,* an unlucky craft which he built for Burton, of Stalham. This wherry seemed to labour under a most comprehensive curse; shortly after being built she sank for no apparent reason, and on another occasion when being quanted against the end of the ebb tide below the Haven Bridge at Yarmouth she struck a steamer's propeller, one blade of which cut through the planking. The gash was stopped up with sacking and later repaired. Yet another mishap occurred when she was moored alongside the wherry *Lord Roberts* in Yarmouth harbour; a paddle tug passed out to sea and her wash broke some of the mooring ropes and lifted the bows of the *Ceres* against the *Lord Roberts,* splitting some of her planks. In 1910 the *Ceres* sank at Yarmouth and had to be raised by two lifting lighters so that she could be pumped out by the steam tug *George Jewson* after her cargo of grain in bags had been removed.

Sometimes wherries were built by a single man working alone or with little help. One of these craftsmen who worked on his own was Ben Benns, who built the *Lord Roberts* just mentioned at Somerton. He is said to have taken three years to complete her, for he was doing other work at the same time and was not employed on her building all the time. He must have done his work well, for the *Lord Roberts* is still in existence; in 1970 she was given to the Norfolk Wherry Trust and it is planned that she should form the centrepiece of a proposed Broadland museum.

Yarmouth produced its wherries as well as its smacks and other sea-going vessels, and many a wherry was launched from the busy yards of this seaport town. The last wherry to be built on the eastern side of the river was the *Ena May,* built by Richard Wooden in the summer of 1895 in his yard near Friars Lane, just to the north of where the town's South Gates used to stand, while the last to be built at Southtown,

The yard of Cox Brothers at Barton Turf, with a transom-sterned wherry hauled out for repair.

on the western bank of the river, was the *Crowhurst*. Her builders were Bessey & Palmer, who were also responsible for much larger vessels such as the schooner barge *Enterprise*, and she was owned successively by John Bass, the General Steam Navigation Company, who changed her name to *Fir* in accordance with their custom of naming vessels after trees, and by one of the Thains.

The ironpots were also built at Southtown, by Fellows. The *Uranus, Vega* and *Sirius* were built for Woods, Sadd, Moore & Co. of Loddon and the *Crystal* for Crisp of Beccles, who used her in the Bungay trade. The builder's specification of the latter vessel is of considerable interest: it shows that she had a length, exclusive of the rudder, of 52 foot, a beam of 15 foot and moulded depth of 3 foot 6 inches; the keel was 6 inches deep, of $\frac{3}{8}$ inch plate, and the plating was of $\frac{3}{16}$ inch steel, while the deck was of wood.

A fifth steel wherry, the *Cygnus*, was built by Fellows "on spec" and was renamed *Diamond* when bought by the Great Yarmouth Shipping Company, who named their craft after precious and semi-precious stones.

Another Yarmouth builder was Billy Barber, who turned out the *Surprise,* later to be converted to a pleasure wherry under the name of *Beta*. He owned this wherry for some time himself, and also built the *Go Forward* for W. H. Thaxter, a Yarmouth owner. One of Barber's wherries is said to have been intended as a rival for the famous racer *Fawn,* but although all right on the wind she had no floor and did not sail well off the wind.

Probably the most famous of all the Yarmouth-built wherries was the 80-ton *Wonder*, which was built for William "Dilly" Smith, the licensee of the *Suspension Bridge Tavern* up the North River, in 1878. James Benns and Thomas Cossey were responsible for her construction, which took place on a yard close to the owner's public house, from which she was launched sideways into the Bure. The *Wonder* is said to have been the only wherry for which a foresail was ever made, which may explain her description being given in the Mercantile Navy List as "cutter."

The *Wonder* was the biggest wherry ever built, but some of the finest and fastest wherries came from Reedham, where members of the Hall family turned out a succession of wherries for trading and pleasure up to 1906 or later.

Charles Hall, like many another member of the waterside fraternity, played a double role, being landlord of the *Brickmakers' Arms* as well as a boatbuilder. His brother James, who had his own yard not far away, was licensee of the *Lord Nelson.*

From the yard of Charles Hall came the *Fawn,* renowned for her success in the wherry races which used to be a feature of many a regatta; though she came from Charles's yard it was Tom Hall, Charles's cousin, who always claimed with pride that he had designed and built her. She was a comparatively small wherry, a 24-tonner with a length of 56 foot and a beam of 15 foot 2 inches. It was difficult to stow cargo in her as she was so finely built, with no flatness of floor, but she won many prizes for her owner, Isaac Wales, the Reedham timber merchant, until she became a pleasure wherry. In that role she proved by no means as fast, and she was eventually broken up on Darby's Hard at Gorleston after having sunk near Acle Dyke.

A contrast in hull form was the *Bell,* another wherry built by Hall for Wales. She was launched on June 21st, 1895, and at the end of October the same year she was sold to Walter Bunn, of Yarmouth, taking her first freight of bricks for him on November 1st. Bunn also owned the 40-ton *Maud,* built by Hall in 1900, and the *Shamrock,* another 40-tonner and the last trading wherry built at the Halls' yard, in 1902. These wherries later went to the Yare & Waveney Lighter Co. Ltd., which sold them in 1918 to J. S. Hobrough.

From Halls' yard also came several pleasure wherries, including the *Claudian* of 1889 which finished up on top of a drifter hulk on Lake Lothing during the 1953 floods. The *Solace* was built there by Daniel Hall, Charles's son, in 1903 and the *Hathor* was built for the Misses Ethel and Helen Colman in 1905. Next year came the counter-sterned *Ecila* ("Alice" spelt backwards) later renamed *Sundog,* and now being restored to sailing trim after many years as an unrigged houseboat.

Wherries were built at Norwich, too. During the first half of the nineteenth century several seagoing vessels were built at Carrow, and there are paintings of the same period which show wherries hauled out at a small yard there. Henry Gallant built the *Fanny* in 1853 on a Carrow yard, possibly the same yard on which Thomas Batley had built bigger vessels twenty or thirty years earlier, and Stephen Field had a yard a little further downstream at Thorpe on which he built a number of wherries. This yard is reputed to have been in the hands of the Field family for about 200 years, but it was taken over by another family on Stephen Field's death about 1890.

Near the heart of the city were Petch's Docks, on the bend of the river at Pockthorpe opposite the Cow Tower. William Murrell Petch was licensee of the busy *Horse Barracks* public house in Barrack Street as well as boatbuilder, but he seems to have combined two jobs without detriment to the extent of his trade. One of the wherries built at his yard was the *Jessie,* of 1860, and another was the *Caroline,* and it was in these "docks" that Petch used to repair the "gas wherries" that supplied the Norwich gasworks with coal.

The last wherry completed at Norwich was the 40-ton *Enchantress,* built on a yard a little way below Foundry Bridge on the site later occupied by Ranson's timberyard. She was not the last wherry to be launched at Norwich, however, for she was followed by the *Unknown,* built by Mollett Brothers in a cut between the Devil's Tower and the old Carrow Bridge, which was some distance downstream of the present bridge. For some reason she was launched before completion and taken to Reedham for fitting out.

A sawpit at Catfield in 1938. Every wherry building yard had its sawpit for cutting out the strakes.

It is said that she acquired the name *Unknown* because in fact she was given no name by her first owner, who used her to collect barley from malthouses on the North River for delivery to Bullard's brewery at Norwich, or to bring to the city cargoes of grain loaded from ships at Yarmouth. Later when owned by Edward J. Edwards she was named, appropriately, the *Macadam,* as she was employed mainly in the carrying of flint and stones for road repairs, landing these at convenient staithes throughout the area. This wherry had higher right-ups and flatter hatches than most wherries, and was also provided with unusually closely spaced timbers; there was only about a handspan between each. Like the *Jessie* and *Caroline* and many another wherry, the *Macadam* was eventually laid to rest in a dyke near Hobrough's Dock at Thorpe.

Some of the little yards that existed on the Norfolk rivers may never have built a wherry, but many of them carried out a lot of wherry repair work in between building of reed barges and other small craft. When wherries needed an overhaul a fixed sum was charged for the use of the tackle and a "hauling out allowance" in the form of beer had to be provided by the owner as soon as the boat was out of the water; the allowance was served out by the wherryman among the men who had worked the windlass or assisted in the work in any way; sometimes those who had assisted only by looking on managed to get a share as well.

When the bottoms of wherries or reed boats needed retarring the boatwrights used a "shoof" of reed to burn the old tar off the hull so it could be scraped clean before applying a fresh coat with a long-handled brush. The wherryman stayed on or about his craft all the time it was on the yard, looking after his master's interests. He also employed his time in scraping the mast, oiling and painting the blocks and overhauling the sail and rigging.

There is in existence a most interesting bill for the repair of the wherry *Leveret,*

Petch's Docks opposite the Cow Tower at Norwich in the early years of this century.

Repairing wherries at Hall's yard at Reedham about 1900.

owned by Norwich coal merchant William England. It records repairs carried out on the yard of Richard Purdy at Coldham Hall in 1909: the cost of labour for three men amounted to £13 8s. for a total of 53½ man-days; painting, three coats, and varnish came to £3; an item for oakum, pitch, tar and mops came to £1 10s.; and with the cost of timber used and five fathom of reed, presumably for burning off the old tar, the total bill amounted to £21 5s. 3d.

Though there was no regular building yard established at Rockland wherries were often hauled out on the hard ground on the east side of the dyke leading up to the staithe and were refitted by a local man, aided by two others who came from Yarmouth. One wherry was built on the west side of the dyke for the landlord of the Rockland New Inn, William Watson, who also carried on business as a coal merchant; his family consisted of four boys, so the wherry was named *The Brothers*.

Perhaps the best known of all wherry builders was William Brighton, remembered today almost solely as the builder of the Norfolk Wherry Trust's *Albion,* though in the course of a long career he turned out a variety of craft. He began building boats at Bungay when in his teens, producing a lateener, the *Ariel,* in 1861. Two years later he built the wherry *Waveney* at Duke's Bridge on the Bungay-Beccles road about half-way between the town of Bungay and Wainford Mills, some distance from the river whose name she was given. She was taken across the marshes on rollers to her launching, but when he built his second wherry, the *Blanche,* on Honeypot Meadow, Bungay, she was carried through the streets on a trolley and launched sideways into a dyke. The *Waveney* subsequently became Di Thain's *Eva Rosa,* was finally converted to a pleasure wherry under the name of *Black Prince,* and was broken up on Allen's yard at Coltishall after ending her days as a motor wherry.

By 1865 he had moved to Norwich, where he built the yawl *Otter* in that year and the schooner *Emerald* five years later. Lengthened by him in 1872 and again altered

121

four years after that, she passed into German ownership as the *Loreley* and was fitted with a "gasoline motor" in 1902. We also find him building at Brundall and at Surlingham, where in 1871 he launched a fishing lugger for Yarmouth, but by 1875 he was at Yarmouth, where he constructed a succession of vessels, including a pleasure wherry, the *Waveney,* in 1891.

He later moved from Yarmouth to Oulton Broad, where his yard was on the saltwater side of the lock. It was here that he built the *Albion* in 1898. Besides building yachts he designed a number which were built by other people, and there are still several of his half-models in existence. One of them, in the Bridewell Museum at Norwich, is of unusual interest because a letter pasted on the back of the baseboard throws light on the methods of yacht designers and builders of the late nineteenth century.

Addressed to J. Wynne, of Herringfleet, and dated 1884, it is "in reply to yours respecting river four Toner". Brighton goes on to say "I can make you a model and grave you the Lines ... the Price would acordint to the state it is got up viz from 2£ to 5 acrdent to finish if you wish for the designs of a 5 Ton yacht and all moulds and Bevels of Timbers the Price £10 10s." Research has failed to reveal the name of the yacht of which this is a model, and it is possible that no boat was in fact built to this design, for in 1886 William A. S. Wynne, of St. Olave's Priory, Herringfleet, had the cutter *Spartan* built at Wivenhoe by J. E. Wilkins to a design by G. L. Watson; possibly this was the boat he was thinking of when he asked Brighton to quote a price for designing a yacht.

Brighton made a half-model when designing the *Albion*, yet despite his unusual effort the *Albion's* lines were by no means as graceful as those of many another wherry. It is said that W. D. & A. E. Walker, for whom she was built, stipulated that she should be carvel planked as it was felt that this would be an advantage when going through

A wherry hauled out for repair on Darby's yard at Beccles.

the locks up to Bungay; maybe they had had experience of the lands of the clinker planking of other wherries catching the rough brick walls of some locks.

William Brighton was not the only man to build wherries at Bungay, for W. D. & A. E. Walker had a private yard there. From that yard came the *Eudora* in 1890, built by John Winter, and the *Iolanthe* in 1892, built by George Davey. Both these craft were sold by Walkers' to Watney, Combe, Reid & Co. Ltd. in 1920, passing to the General Steam Navigation Company six years later. The name of the *Iolanthe* then became *Elder*, and she was still afloat in the 1950s, when May Gurney of Trowse were using her for carrying mud from their dredgers. The *Eudora* continued under her original name until she fell a victim to incendiary bombs during an air raid on Norwich during the second world war.

Nor was he by any means the only one to build wherries at Lowestoft and Oulton Broad. Lucas Brothers had a yard on the south side of Lowestoft harbour on which they built a number of wherries, and Robert Kemp built wherries, including pleasure wherries, at Oulton Broad.

Before bringing into use their own yard at Bungay Staithe Walkers' used to have their wherries periodically pulled out and overhauled at Wright's yard in Northgate, Beccles. The last wherry built at this yard was the 40-ton *Emerald*, ordered by Crisps of Beccles about 1880 to replace the *Garnet*, which was too wide to pass through the old Beccles bridge. George Wright was still describing himself as "barge and boat builder" a good many years later, however.

That unconventional nineteenth-century yachtsman Edward Fitzgerald had a 16 foot half-decked yacht, the *Waveney*, built at Beccles by one of the Wrights in 1860, and a very good little craft she seems to have been. Her boatman, Ted West, is said to have remarked "She'll do all but speak" and at Aldeburgh a sailor told Old Fitz "She go like a wiolin, she do," a remark which pleased her owner greatly.

When the *Waveney* was laid up after her first season her keel bolts were found to be defective, however. We might ignore such a shortcoming on the part of the builder were it not for the light which Fitz's remarks throw on wherry building at this period and on the character of this Beccles boatbuilder. In a letter written from Geldeston in February, 1862, FitzGerald said: "I have been twice to old Wright, who has built a Boat of about 14 feet on speculation and has laid down the Keel of a new wherry, on speculation also. But he has as yet no Orders, and thinks his business is like to be very slack ... I showed him two of the guilty Screws which had almost let my Leaden Keel part from the wooden one: he says he had desired the Smith not to make *too* large heads, and the Smith accordingly made them too small; and some Apprentice had, he supposes, fixed them in without further inspection. There is such honesty and cheerfulness in Wright's Saxon Eyes and Countenance when he faces such a charge as disarms all one's wrath."

CHAPTER EIGHT

Water Frolics and Regattas

YACHTING on the Broads did not begin merely in the 1870s and 1880s when visitors began to explore the region. In fact it is impossible to say just when the first pleasure boat was built, but by the beginning of the nineteenth century there were certainly some such craft making their way round the water frolics.

Undoubtedly some of these water frolics were, as the name perhaps suggests, little more than rustic amusements in which the marshmen would sail their punts and the watermen would compete in rowing and quanting races, but those which attained a mention in the newspapers of the day were great social occasions attended by the gentry from miles around.

In the latter part of the eighteenth century Beccles Water Frolic was being held on Oulton Broad and Burgh Water Frolic, attended annually by the Mayor of Yarmouth, was already an ancient institution. It was traditional for the Mayor and Corporation to walk in procession from the Town Hall to the quay, there to embark in a wherry "purposefully fitted up for their accommodation and plentifully stored." Year after year one reads of how the Mayor and his retinue led a fleet to the head of Breydon, there to feast on board their "barge" while the sportsmen raced their craft the more keenly, no doubt, for the wagers that had been made on the results of the matches.

One year we read of "a sumptuous dinner, provided by the Mayor," being laid out in the hold of the Mayor's wherry, while another year we note the report of "wherries crammed with comestibles internally, the freights of innkeepers and others ... and externally loaded with human beings" having joined the excursion.

Usually all went well and everyone thoroughly enjoyed the "aquatic amusements," but at the 1863 event the hatches of the wherry *Ruby,* being used as a floating grand-stand, gave way as the passengers crowded to one side to see the winner of a well-contested race cross the finishing line. The nine who were flung overboard seem to have escaped with nothing worse than a ducking, but two unfortunates who were looking out from beneath the hatches were almost decapitated as the wooden hatch covers fell on them.

Perhaps this double fatality gave the ancient frolic a bad name; however that may be, the event declined in succeeding years, and though revived with all the old ceremony and hospitality by F. Danby Palmer in 1888 it failed to survive the century.

A wherry race at Barton regatta; left to right, *Despatch, Cornucopia* and *Ella*.

A double drowning at Wroxham Water Frolic in 1808 did not settle a death spell on that event, however, for two years after the capsize that led to the death of a local farmer and his twelve-year-old nephew no fewer than "one hundred sail of boats" were crowded on Wroxham Broad for the racing.

In 1820, indeed, the *Norfolk Chronicle and Norwich Gazette* reported that "a greater number of pleasure-boats of all kinds were assembled on this beautiful broad than on any former occasion." It must have been quite a date in the social calendar at that period, for "there was an unusual display of fashionable company present to witness this aquatic fête," including a number of titled gentlemen in the *Rob Roy*. It was not a day entirely given over to the entertainment of the upper classes, however, for "numbers of wherries, laden with country folks in their holiday clothes, added much to the cheerfulness of the scene and the interest of the whole spectacle."

There was as yet, though, no race for wherries. The competition seems to have been confined to pleasure boats of various kinds and various rigs.

If we are to believe the evidence of such artists as James Stark, some of the smaller craft of this period were rigged with spritsails. The sprit rig was a very handy one for

125

small vessels and was widely used for working craft as well as pleasure boats years ago, though it has survived to modern times only in the big barges of the Thames Estuary. As H. C. Folkard said in his book *The Sailing Boat*, "for small open sailing boats, there is no better, safer, nor more convenient rig than the sprit-sail and fore-sail; and to a tyro boat-sailor it is recommended as superior to many others, for boats under eighteen feet in length."

The bigger pleasure boats of the Norfolk waterways were cutter rigged, with big gaff mainsails. Such a craft was the *Red Rover,* a well-known racer in her day. The advertisement published in a local newspaper when she was for sale in 1840 gives us a good description of her: 26 foot "on the ram," that is, from stem to sternpost, with a beam of 10 foot 5 inches, and drawing less than 3 foot, "fitted with commodious 9 foot covered cabin and 8 foot Stern Sheets with benches and lockers around and handsome copper rail, copper fastenings, copper bolts and bands throughout, with lead keel, about 1 ton of iron Ballast ... The Red Rover is universally admitted to be the fastest and handsomest Boat on the Stream; her Cabin is fitted with sleeping berths and hair mattress, and has a mahogany dining table with additional leaves and drawers, painted floor cloth, copper cooking stove, and every requisite for a first-class Boat for the Season."

In such a craft the early Victorian gentleman cruised from one water frolic to another in order to pit his boat and the racing know-how of his professional skipper against those of other sportsmen.

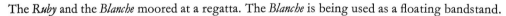

The *Ruby* and the *Blanche* moored at a regatta. The *Blanche* is being used as a floating bandstand.

The pleasure wherry *Solace* sailing in a wherry race at Wroxham Regatta in 1910.

Many of the racing craft of the nineteenth century were not cutter rigged but lateen, however. One wonders how this rig came to be used in Norfolk, so far from the Mediterranean and the Red Sea, normally considered to be the home of the lateen sail. There is a story that the lateen rig was introduced to East Anglia by an officer returned from a spell of duty in Malta; it might equally well have been introduced by the master of some Yarmouth brigantine trading out to Naples with barrelled herring or sailing to Smyrna after fruit, who reckoned that this sail which served so well on the tartanes and caiques would take a pleasure boat to the fore of any sailing match on the Yare or the Waveney.

Though we cannot say how the lateen sail came to these waters, we do know that by the 1820s the sportsmen of Norfolk and Suffolk had adopted the lateen rig for many of their pleasure boats. At that time the boats were rigged with two lateen sails, as one can see on some of Stark's pictures, painted about 1830. Development gave later craft a lugsail on the mizzen mast, which was placed only a little aft of amidships, while some of the larger lateeners set a big gaffsail on this second mast. The foremast raked forward over the bows; the great lateen sail was carried on a yard nearly 40 foot long, almost twice the length of the boat, and was laced at the foot to a boom.

127

"This rig is admirably adapted for narrow waters and rivers, where short tacking is unavoidable," says Folkard. "Boats for turning to windward in narrow channels must be short and wide; a long rakish craft is unmanageable in such waters. The river Yare in Norfolk may boast of some of the fastest and prettiest boats, after this rig, of any in England: the largest are twenty six feet on the ram, and ten feet beam; the smaller size are sixteen feet on deck, while the breadth of beam is eight feet six inches."

Under the pull of that enormous lateen sail the lateener was a fast craft. It was unfortunate, however, that in fitting the rig to local conditions the Norfolk builders raked the foremast forward, for in that position the big sail tended to push the head of the craft down; the sail of the dhow on its aft-raking mast, on the other hand, was a lifting sail. Beating into wind was the best point of sailing, but running before the wind could be extremely dangerous work as the towering foresail posed right over the bows forced the boat's head deep into the water. Sometimes in spite of the whole crew being gathered on the counter to bring their weight as far aft as possible, a lateener would drive under, fill and sink.

What a sight it was to see such boats racing. "How these boats roared through the water when manoeuvring to take up position, heeling right over beneath their 40 foot spars till even keels could sometimes be seen," wrote Oliver Ready in his *Life and Sport on the Broads*. "It was most exciting, but suddenly they were all in a beautiful line, with snow-white sails fluttering and cracking like whips in the gale, when 'Bang!' went the starting gun, and they were off.

"At the report the old *Thorn* seemed to shoot right ahead, gaining a lead of perhaps forty yards within the first half-minute, and there she stuck for the whole race, with the other eight boats hard on her heels like a pack of hounds, leaving behind them lanes of foam and sending up a combined roar that carried to the furthest limits of the broad. You never saw such a sight! The poor old *Thorn* looked just like a hunted deer, settling down into the water as though straining every nerve to escape, while each minute our hearts were in our mouths as she staggered wildly beneath her towering spread of canvas."

The *Thorn* came in twenty yards ahead of the cutter yacht which proved to be her main rival in this race, winning six beautiful silver salt-cellars in a silk-lined leather case. But the cutter had given a taste of her quality, and that memorable race, says Ready, sounded the knell of the picturesque but somewhat dangerous and cumbersome lateen rig.

Some of the lateeners were rebuilt as cutters, but a few continued to race under their original rig until near the end of the century. One, the 11-ton *Ariel,* built at Bungay in 1861 by William Brighton, was still sailing the Broads under her great lateen sail in the opening decade of the present century, having received a new suit of sails as late as 1896.

No other lateener survived for so long as the famous *Maria,* built at Yarmouth in 1827 and bought some ten years later by Sir Jacob Preston, who owned and sailed her for a full fifty years. The man for whom she was built, a Mr. J. Plowman, of Normanstone, Lowestoft, had an earlier lateener named *Maria* which he raced at Burgh Water Frolic in the early 1820s; probably this is the small lateener with this name to be seen on the engraving of Mutford Bridge in Stark's "River Scenery."

Sir Jacob was a great sailing man, and under his ownership the *Maria* soon became known as a swift and successful racer, building up an enviable reputation as the fastest boat on the Broads. There is a story that once at Wroxham regatta the other competitors refused to sail against the invincible *Maria* and Sir Jacob had to withdraw her. All the same, it was an exciting race, but it was followed by even greater excitement when the *Maria's* crew boarded the winner, the lateener *Hornet.* In the free-for-all that followed the man who held the disputed cup was thrown overboard and the cup sank to the bottom of the broad.

In 1888 a yachtsman on a Broads cruise noted in his log that "one of the sights of the day, I consider, was seeing old Sir Jacob Preston in the *Maria,* sailing his own boat all over the Broad just as I have seen him doing years ago. The same boat, the same rig, the same master, now 80 years of age. It was worth going up the North River to see such a reminder of old times..."

"The old Black Maria," as George Christopher Davies always called her, continued to sail the Broadland rivers up to the outbreak of war in 1914. She was seen at Barton regatta that year, but after the regatta she was returned to her boathouse and after the war was dismantled. She never left that thatched boathouse again until 1969, when she was taken to the Maritime Museum for East Anglia at Yarmouth, where she is now on exhibition.

By the middle of the nineteenth century, by a curious coincidence at almost the same time that the sportsmen were getting together to found the first yacht clubs in the area, the watermen were emulating the yachtsmen and were racing their wherries at some of the regattas. In 1852, seven years before the establishment of the premier yacht club on the Broads, a pair of silver-mounted horns was offered as a prize at Wroxham regatta "to be sailed for by Wherries not exceeding 20 tons, no quants or boat hooks allowed."

Seven years later the wherrymen racing at Wroxham regatta competed for a first prize of five guineas, the second craft getting thirty shillings and the third ten shillings. "This match will not take place unless the wherries are at their moorings, ready to start, beside the Reed House, by 10.30 a.m. Entrance fee, two shillings." Thus reads the advertisement which appeared in the local newspaper a few days before the regatta. Does that condition hint at some intransigence on the part of wherrymen at an earlier regatta, I wonder?

Be that as it may, the race took place and was won by the *Sarah Ann,* owned by William Warnes of Somerton. The *Elizabeth,* a craft owned by Robert Crowe, of Horning, came second, with the *Alma,* owned by James Riches, of Palling, a close third.

The wherry race seems to have been the main event before lunch. Having satisfied the lusty watermen, no doubt, the more genteel yachtsmen could get on with their own racing in the afternoon unhampered by the preparations of the rival wherry skippers. As it was, many people were up early in the morning making ready for the regatta.

Mr Green of Wroxham had very neatly decorated one of his commodious wherries, having the hatches heightened. The inside was lined with white, trimmed with red, and adorned with evergreens and flowers for the accommodation of a large party of friends. In the course of the forenoon this craft, attached to which was a boat containing Fitzgerald's brass band, proceeded up the beautiful winding stream leading to the Broad, the band playing 'Rule Britannia.'

After this followed other wherries with their numerous living freights, on board one of which was the old fiddler, Gipsey Gray, performing almost an innumerable quantity of reels and hornpipes to the delight of his auditory.

What a delightful day that must have been.

From that time on wherry races were a feature of regattas on Wroxham, Barton and Hickling Broads, Horsey Mere, Breydon, Oulton Broad and possibly at other centres such as Cantley. There were also wherry races at Yarmouth Roads Regatta from 1882 onwards, at Lowestoft Marine Regatta from 1883, and at Gorleston Marine Regatta from 1885.

Whenever wherry racing was talked of the name of the *Fawn,* one of the craft owned by Isaac Wales, of Reedham, was sure to be mentioned. She had perhaps the most consistent success of any wherry and Wales took a considerable pride in her

The lateener *Maria* on Barton Broad in 1914.

achievements; her skipper, "Ophir" Powley, used to carry a basket of homing pigeons with him when racing at sea, and one would be sent off at the end of each round with a message for the waiting owner at home in Reedham.

The *Fawn* was the winner of the first wherry race at Lowestoft, the entry of ten in that race being the largest number that ever competed there. She won in the five succeeding years, but between 1888 and 1895 there was no racing for the wherries at Lowestoft. In 1895 the wherry race was reinstated in the programme and the *Fawn* was first home again, but she lost the prize as a result of a protest from her two competitors, the *Hope* and the *Surprise,* that she passed the Pakefield mark boat on the wrong side. It was blowing very hard, and the wherries had to gybe round the turning point. No doubt fearing that his mast would not stand the strain of a gybe, her skipper luffed the *Fawn* round; the *Hope,* however, took the very heavy gybe without damage and the *Surprise* eased her peak and also got round successfully.

Wales had the *Olga* built by one of the Halls in 1896, and the *Fawn* had to take second place to her at Wroxham regatta that year. At Lowestoft in the same year these two were the only entrants, but so much interest was taken in the rivalry between the 21-year-old *Fawn* and the new wherry that the committee waived the rule of "three to start or no race" so that they might fight it out.

The *Olga* got away first, but by the end of the first round the *Fawn* was in the lead. She held her position for two rounds, but in the last round she was overtaken by the *Olga.*

The *Fawn* competed once more at Lowestoft, in 1898, but in that race she had to be content with third place, the *Olga* leading the *Dora* home by only 33 seconds, a little more than three minutes ahead of the *Fawn.*

It was the second of this series of wherry races at Lowestoft that provided a first-class sensation for the spectators. Two of the eight wherries competing collided at the end of the first round, one of them, the *Ellen,* belonging to John Goff, of Loddon, sinking in about three minutes. Her crew of eight (racing seems to have required many more hands than trading) were thrown into the sea, but were rescued by the other wherry involved, the *Robert Alfred,* which belonged to Robert Pratt of Yarmouth. The fault seems to have lain with the latter, for Goff later obtained judgment in the County Court against her owner. Two days after the collision the *Ellen* was hauled on to Lowestoft North Beach, and the master was able to retrieve his cash and two watches from the cabin. No doubt he was very glad indeed to recover the £14 he had left on board, but the watches can have been little use after a couple of days in salt water.

The last wherry races at Lowestoft Marine Regatta were sailed in 1899 and 1901, and the *Dora,* with neither the *Fawn* nor the *Olga* against her, won them both. In the last race the *Maud* was second, followed by the *Bell.*

A wherry race was advertised in 1902, but it never took place. Exactly what happened on regatta day is not clear; the *Albion* and *Maud* passed through the swing bridge intending to race, but there was some trouble and the race did not come off. Probably the committee invoked the rule that four were to start or there would be no race, but wherrymen ever afterwards spoke of an argument about prizes, saying that the masters of the wherries were dissatisfied and refused to start.

That was the end of racing at sea, for though the *Dora* had led the *Maud* home at Yarmouth that year no more wherry races were held. The last wherry race at Gorleston had been sailed ten years earlier.

But it was certainly not the end of wherry racing, for races for both trading and pleasure wherries continued to be a feature of some of the inland regattas until the 1930s. In the end Barton regatta was the last to include a race for wherries, though there were two races on Breydon, in 1952 and 1953. The first year the *Albion,* by then taken over by the Norfolk Wherry Trust, broke her mast; the second year she sailed home alone after the pleasure wherry *Dragon,* her sole rival, had withdrawn from the race.

Though the punts still raced on Barton Broad and the cruisers still had races elsewhere, most of the regattas were dominated by the dinghy classes, sailing under rules which were very different in many respects from those under which the lateeners had raced a century before. The regattas had changed greatly, and there was no longer a place for the working craft, even had there still been any to take part in the racing.

Late nineteenth-century yachts on the Broads. The rig of the boat on the right is a variation, or perhaps a development, of that of the lateener.

CHAPTER NINE

A'pleasuring

NOBODY seems able to say for certain when the idea of making the hold of a wherry into a number of cabins and using the vessel for pleasure purposes was first thought of. The practice certainly became popular enough when the Broads began to attract men and women in search of an out-of-the-ordinary holiday about the 1880s.

There had been pleasure boats and pleasure barges in use on the Norfolk and Suffolk rivers back in the eighteenth century, if not before, but it seems unlikely that the first wherry to be fitted up for a cruise was commissioned until about 1860. It was around this date that the Rev. T. A. Wheeler and Mr. Gambling of Buxton Mills on the upper Bure took part in a cruise in a wherry owned by the latter. The hold was swept and garnished for the cruise of three weeks or so, and at its close the wherry reverted to trading. The Rev. T. A. Wheeler was the father of Dr. Wheeler, who became known intimately to later generations as the headmaster of Bracondale School, Norwich. Born in 1852, young Wheeler himself took part in the cruise.

William Cooke, the Stalham miller and corn merchant, is also said to have either built or converted a wherry for pleasure at about this time, but Walter Rye's old skipper, Tungate, who was born about 1811, used to think that the first pleasure wherry he saw was the *Triumph* of Wroxham, which was covered in by the manual labour of two rather remarkable men, "Parson" Blake, otherwise the Rev. Francis Jex Blake of Swanton Abbot, who died in 1908, and his cousin "Captain" Blake, who was an officer in the merchant service. Both were tall, strong men and they sailed their craft, which had been built at Coltishall by H. Press in 1860, without professional help. The *Triumph* had only two cabins and was very roughly fitted with mattresses, a table and gun racks only, yet "Parson" Blake often spent a good part of the winter on board.

When the Broads were "discovered" an enterprising owner of trading wherries conceived the idea of converting his craft into pleasure wherries and letting them to parties of holiday-makers during the summer months. Who first did this it is hard to say, but Press Brothers of North Walsham were at least among the pioneers; in 1888 they advertised the wherries *Bertha, Elsie, Kate, Diligent* and *Lucy* for hire. They had two cabins, one for ladies and the other for gentlemen, the latter serving as a dining saloon in the daytime. It was stated in the advertisement that three or four ladies and four to six gentlemen could be accommodated.

The hatches of the wherries were raised, sides were fitted complete with windows

An Edwardian pleasure party on the *Reindeer*.

on top of the standing right-ups and the holds were partitioned and furnished fairly comfortably. It was simple to strip the furnishings and replace the shifting right-ups when the wherries reverted to trading during the winter. The cabins had blinds, soft cushions and plenty of rugs, but a piano cost an extra fifteen shillings a week. Parties were required, according to the advertisement, to go on board wherever the owners might desire, but they could leave at any place convenient to themselves by giving a week's notice.

In the same year J. Jimpson of Wroxham had the wherry *Enchantress* for hire, and G. Applegate and W. Knight of Potter Heigham were also advertising that they each had a wherry for hire. They appeared among a comparatively short list of yacht hirers who possessed also cutter-rigged yachts of various sizes and lugsail boats, all for the convenience and amusement of visitors.

134

Eleven years later Harry Adcock of Beccles announced that he had the *Zoe,* which had been built by Robert Harrison at Ludham in 1873, and that she "is not used at any period of the year for trading purposes." This apparently was intended to signify that she was more comfortable than those only temporarily converted; certainly she was panelled throughout with polished English oak, of which material her fittings were made, and the ladies' cabin was fitted with two brass bedsteads, wire spring mattresses and so on, and there was a water supply laid on.

Also in a list published by the Great Eastern Railway Company in 1899 were the *Bertha, Kate, Ethnie* and *Diligent,* owned by Press & Pallett of North Walsham, successors of Press Brothers, who also advertised the nine-ton cutter yacht *Myth.* Ling & Company, Gambling's successors at Buxton Mills, who had the *Britannia* and another *Bertha,* announced that "a piano is on board each yacht." The piano seems to have been as important to the Victorian and Edwardian yachtsman as his radio set is to the

The *Bertha,* one of the early conversions. She has her bonnet laced on to the foot of the sail.

135

A counter-sterned pleasure wherry at Yarmouth.   The *Hathor* crossing Breydon in a fresh wind.

present-day holidaymaker in his motor cruiser. At Oxnead Mills, a few miles higher up the Bure, C. Browne had the wherries *Volunteer* and *Enterprise,* which probably carried cargoes of grain for their miller owner during the winter season.

The *Victory,* with three cabins providing accommodation for seven or eight people, was advertised by R. Collins & Son of Wroxham, while other wherries with three cabins were advertised by J. E. Bullen of Oulton Broad, who had the *Victoria* and *Elbe.* Other Oulton Broad owners were R. Kemp & Company, who had the *British Queen,* a product of one of the Halls of Reedham, which was stated to be a "first-rate fast pleasure wherry of about 28 tons" and to have been the winner of a first prize at Wroxham Regatta in 1896. Her saloon was panelled in mahogany and sequoia pine.

A bathroom was among the attractions of the 35-ton *Rambler,* built in 1898, which was offered by A. R. Brown of Cobholm. More comfortable than the older craft, she had a saloon and three sleeping cabins providing accommodation for ten or twelve people. Brown also had the *Herald,* a wherry of 22 tons offering accommodation for eight or ten people.

"The fine new pleasure wherry *Industry*" of 26 tons was offered for hire by another Yarmouth owner, G. R. Bateley, at his boat station on the North Quay.

Like the larger yachts, the pleasure wherries were let with a skipper to sail them and a steward to cook and wait on the holidaymakers. As the steward was usually a waterman he served also as mate.

The earliest of these pleasure wherries may have been only humble trading craft with their holds cleaned out and furnished, but it did not take long for somebody to see the advantages of a wherry specially built as a pleasure craft. The wherry was so well adapted to the rivers on which she had her birth that the hull form and the sail needed no alteration, but the interior could be made more palatial, could be laid out more conveniently and furnished more sumptuously, and the finish could be improved. Red and blue paint could be dispensed with and varnish could take its place.

While some of the converted wherries, even when they no longer reverted to trading in winter, retained the chain plates on their right-ups, like the *Violet,* which kept this feature to the end, no such reminder of mundane workaday trials troubled the holidaymaker on the later pleasure wherries. When the *Claudian* was built by Charles Hall at Reedham in 1887 men came from Norwich to fit out the interior, and the *Hathor,* built by Charles's son Daniel Hall in 1905, had inlaid panelling in the saloon which was a very far cry from the pine ceiling of the first pleasure wherry conversions.

The *Claudian* was the first wherry to be built exclusively for letting out to parties for cruising on the Broads. Earlier conversions had been ballasted with iron weights in the bilge, but the *Claudian* had a three-ton lead keel fitted.

A rather later pleasure wherry intended specially for the hiring trade was the *Dragon,* built at Wroxham in 1901 by the Norfolk Broads Yachting Co. Ltd., a firm which came into existence to cater for the holidaymakers who flocked to the Broads after reading books and articles by George Christopher Davies, Harry Brittain and other early Broads writers. The company gave up business in 1920, its premises at Potter Heigham being taken over by Walter Woods while at Wroxham the local manager, Alfred Pegg, continued that part of the business in partnership with his son.

The firm owned three pleasure wherries, and on that fateful day in 1920 the *Dragon,* a big craft of 40 tons, fetched £725; the smaller *Fairy Queen* went for £625 and the *Endeavour,* later to be converted to power under the name of *Darkie,* for £550. That gives one an idea of the value of a pleasure wherry half a century ago.

Hire terms for a wherry about 1910, as given in a list of yachts and boats for hire issued by the Norfolk Broads Yachting Company, were only sixteen guineas for a big wherry like the *Dragon,* and twelve or thirteen guineas for the smaller craft; small yachts could be had for four guineas a week with a waterman in charge or three if the holidaymaker was prepared to sail and look after himself.

These prices were quoted as "during August—prices during other months on application," and even in 1930 when the Broads season had been extended to some degree one could hire a wherry at the height of the season for less than £30 a week, including the pay of the skipper and steward.

For the convenience of passengers many pleasure wherries had a stout seat of the garden variety placed on the foredeck. Here the holiday party could take their ease both when under way and when at moorings, but when a bridge had to be negotiated the seat, like the winch, had to be pushed aside.

The absence of any other convenient deck space on a pleasure wherry was a disadvantage to the holidaymaker, so it is not surprising that one or two owners decided to have their wherries rebuilt with counter sterns. One rather remarkable conversion was the *Zenobia,* formerly the trading wherry *Olive Branch,* built by Allen of Coltishall; not only was she given a counter stern but also a mizzen sail and a fore-sail, turning her into what was quaintly described in Lloyd's Register of Yachts as "wherry and yawl."

The pleasure wherry *Victory* moored in the upper Bure by Lammas Church.

Charles Bardwell

Other counter-sterned wherries included the *Ecila,* which had a counter stern added when converted from a trading wherry. A new pleasure wherry with the same name, also with a counter, was built by Daniel Hall at Reedham in 1906, the internal fittings of the original *Ecila* being transferred to the new hull.

Comfortable and eminently suitable as they were for the Norfolk rivers, the wherries were not everybody's choice. Quite apart from those who wanted small boats in which to cruise alone or with only a single companion, there were people who felt that a black-hulled "barge" was not the thing for a yachting trip. They demanded a "real yacht."

In an effort to marry the undoubted advantages of the wherry rig to the yacht hull the Norfolk and Suffolk boatbuilders developed the wherry yacht, a vessel with a graceful carvel-built hull, counter stern and large well and after-deck providing the pleasure party with somewhere better than the wherry's foredeck to sit in the sun when under way. Although the rig was basically the same as that of a wherry, the single halyard being still brought down to a winch on the tabernacle, some of these craft added a boom to the sail.

Though some of these wherry yachts have sailed their native rivers for more than half a century they are following the wherries into oblivion, for the modern Broads holidaymaker generally prefers a big and boxlike motor cruiser. *White Moth, White Heather, White Rose, Norada, Olive, Goldfinch, Golden Hinde* and *Rambler* were the names of some of these well-remembered craft. The *Rambler,* which had a graceful curved stem in place of the more common vertical stem, could accommodate ten people in four double-berth cabins and a single cabin; the double-berth cabin forward and the single-berth cabin could be made "into one exceptionally large bedroom by taking down portable bulkheads if extra comfort is needed when there is only a small party." There was also a bathroom "with full size bath" and, of course, a piano in the saloon.

When I was young and becoming interested in the Broads I always felt that these craft were more yacht than wherry. Yet even the wherry sometimes had to bow to the holidaymakers' fancies, for there is a story that a pleasure wherry belonging to Ernest Collins of Wroxham was once whitewashed on one side to be photographed for inclusion in the firm's list. Perhaps this was the little carvel-built *Liberty,* for in the 1930s she appeared with her hull white enamelled in deference to those patrons of the firm who believed that a black hull was not sufficiently "yachty."

Although the Norfolk Wherry Trust at one time planned to have a new wherry built either as a consort or as a replacement for the *Albion,* the last wherry built remains the *Ardea,* a very big pleasure wherry built of teak by Leo Robinson at Oulton Broad in 1927 for Howard Hollingsworth, the Lowestoft philanthropist. It is said that the order for the *Ardea* was given largely to relieve a depression in the local boatbuilding industry; however that may be, when the wherry was completed Hollingsworth gave a dinner to which he invited every man who had worked on her, and every man found beside his plate an envelope containing a golden sovereign.

Though her planking was of teak instead of oak and the hull was always varnished instead of being tarred or painted, the *Ardea* was in almost every other respect a typical pleasure wherry. She was very big, though, 65 foot long, plus the length of the rudder, and to ease the work of steering such a large craft she had a small steering wheel fitted to the tiller, working on a curved rack.

Her building occupied a surprisingly short space of time, for the order was placed in December, 1926, the design was worked out in about six weeks and she was ready for handing over, equipped right down to a box of matches, in the following August. She lacked the sweet lines of the traditional wherry, her ugliness being explained by a Norfolk boatbuilder once with the short remark "You can't steam teak."

Hollingsworth kept her for seven years, but then in 1934 he disposed of her to Commander R. G. Lock, from whom he acquired the smaller pleasure wherry *Beta,* formerly the trader *Surprise.* She is said to have taken her name on conversion from the early airship *Beta*, her first owner having been a former airship officer.

Both wherries survived the Second World War. I remember the *Beta,* then in use as a houseboat, being equipped with electric lighting for which the current was generated by a small windmill at the masthead. Then in 1959 the *Ardea* was bought by Harold Dunkerley and was taken to Paris, where she was used to solve her new owner's accommodation problem.

The *Ardea* was not the first wherry to go foreign, for in 1888 Henry Montague Doughty took his pleasure wherry *Gipsy* to Holland and that summer and in succeeding years he explored the Dutch waterways and sailed through Germany, penetrating the European rivers and canals to within a few miles of Prague. No Norfolk wherry can ever have gone so far afield.

Her adventures in Europe are told in two books which Doughty wrote later, *Friesland Meres and through the Netherlands in a Norfolk Wherry* and *Our Wherry in Wendish Lands*. Both can still be found from time to time in second-hand bookshops.

It was in August, 1888, that the *Gipsy* sailed from Wroxham down to Yarmouth where, after four tedious days of strong winds which knocked up a big sea outside, a start was made for Stavoren under tow. The wherry had been well prepared for the crossing with coamings round the cockpit and planks fastened across the windows, but Doughty seems to have spent an anxious time on the tug though the crossing was uneventful enough. From Stavoren the owner and his family set off to explore the meres of Friesland and the canals of the Netherlands.

They found the *Gipsy* ideal for the purpose, able to navigate "the narrow waterways, through locks, under bridges, over shallow meres, against and with the current

The pleasure wherry *Gipsy* on Dutch waterways in company with typical Dutch craft.

of great rivers, and upon the sea; and in scarce any other way could one penetrate districts so remote, known to few even of the city-dwelling Netherlanders themselves."

The *Gipsy* spent the winter of 1888 at Leeuwarden, where Doughty noted that the houses were large "as becomes the Friesch capital; often a tree-bordered canal runs down the middle of a street, sometimes the water washes the house walls; the roadways are all paved with clinkers, the narrower without trottoirs, and all wonderfully clean." In the summer of 1889 the exploration of the Netherlands continued.

Next year she went through the Groningen-Delfzyl canal into the Dollart and on towards Emden. An attempt to get through to the Weser by way of Oldenburg proved abortive because the canal shown on the official German map Doughty was using had never been completed, so the *Gipsy* sailed back to Emden, went to sea again and voyaged to Bremerhaven by way of the German naval base of Wilhemshaven. From Hamburg she went into Mecklenberg, back to Elenschleuse and over the Muritzsee, wintering at Waren.

The voyage into Europe was resumed the following year, the *Gipsy* sailing whenever possible but being towed by track horse, steam kahn or tug at various times. Doughty detested being towed but time was limited; it went against the grain, for instance, when on the way to Potsdam under tow he noted that sailing would have been delightful there.

They were at Potsdam when news reached them of the loss of the pleasure wherry *Elsie* while trying to follow the *Gipsy's* trail. "The *Elsie* was bound for a cruise on Friesland Meres," Doughty wrote. "Her charterer had talked his plans over with me, and I heartily hoped that this second wherry to 'go foreign' would be as lucky as the first. It was a shock to hear that she was lost—foundered in the North Sea while being towed. Her crew were got safe out of her, but the unlucky hirer lost his guns and gear which were not insured as the wherry was." The *Elsie* had been let by Press Brothers for a three-month shooting expedition.

At last Doughty was able to record that "the *Gipsy* had now voyaged through the entire length, from north to south, of the German Empire. The Elbe flowed north from us nearly five hundred miles to the German Ocean, and southwards, only ten miles of its course were between us and the frontier of Austria."

The *Gipsy* remained in Continental waters until 1902, when she was towed back to Yarmouth by the paddle tug *Yare*. Arrangements for her return were made by John Loynes, who at that time had a branch of his boat-letting business at Sneek, in the Netherlands, and she was met at Yarmouth by Tom George, who then had charge of the Yarmouth yacht station. George reconditioned her for further cruising on the Broads and she was acquired by Robert Gurney, who renamed her *Cyclops*.

She sailed the Broads for many a year, eventually getting her old name back, but in due course her age showed and her old timbers became too leaky for further service afloat. Yet even when she said goodbye to the water this most adventurous of wherries was by no means finished; for many years she provided a home for a family, propped up on the bank very near Hobrough's dockyard at Thorpe St. Andrew. Her decks were cemented over in an attempt to keep the rainwater out and she looked very pathetic, yet even in 1950 there was an old couple, "Tiny" Moore and his wife, living aboard the *Gipsy*. "Tiny" has now passed on, and so has the old *Gipsy*.

A typical Victorian pleasure party, all showing clear signs of enjoying their voyage in a pleasure wherry.

CHAPTER TEN

The end of the voyage

W HEN A KEEL or a wherry was no longer sound enough to carry dry cargoes it could still be put to the task of carting mud from the dredgers used to keep the navigable channel clear, and many a once-proud craft ended its days in this way.

William Cubitt, drawing up his plan for a navigation to bring sea-going ships to Norwich, visualised the use of keels "to attend on the dredgers" and the Great Yarmouth Port and Haven Commissioners advertised from time to time for keels to carry away the spoil brought up by their "dredging machines." It was hard and damaging work, but important work nonetheless.

An early Yarmouth "dydelling machine" was operated by horses, but steam power was particularly suitable for harnessing to such work as dredging and when the harbour was being constructed at Lowestoft Jabez Bayley, a well-known Ipswich shipbuilder, was brought in to build a steam dredger for use by the Company of Proprietors of the Norwich and Lowestoft Navigation. This was a curious-looking craft with sash windows and a pedimented Georgian door in its lofty wooden sides

One of the sub-contractors involved in the construction of the Norwich and Lowestoft Navigation was Henry Crosskill Hobrough, who had served his apprenticeship to a boatwright in Southtown and had subsequently become proprietor of a licensed house at Haddiscoe, where on the coming of the railway he also filled the position of stationmaster. He sub-contracted to carry out work on a half-mile section of the Haddiscoe New Cut and was also concerned with the piling of Mutford Lock, linking Oulton Broad with Lake Lothing.

This work seems to have given him a taste for civil engineering, for he later moved to Norwich and set up as a general contractor. His son James became licensee of a public house in Bishopgate, Norwich, and from that establishment carried on an extensive business as a lighterage, dredging and piling contractor.

Remembered for the "wideawake" hat which he always wore, James Hobrough was a man of considerable stature and great strength; he was known once to have carried a 5 cwt. piling bell. "Admiral" Hobrough, as he was always called, died in 1901, forty-seven years after the establishment of James Hobrough & Son, and was succeeded at the head of the firm by his son, James Samuel Hobrough.

The firm had a hand in a great many engineering schemes, lightering soil from the excavations for the Norwich Gas Company's gasholder near Bishop's Bridge and carrying out work on the foundations of the Cantley beet sugar factory. Most of the dredging work on the Norfolk rivers, as well as much weed-cutting and other maintenance work, was carried out by the firm, whose wherries were also used for transporting Norwich refuse from the tips at Fishergate down to Kirby Bedon for disposal on the marshes.

In the 1930s when a floating green weed was spreading rapidly on Hickling Broad, choking the navigation and threatening to reduce the shallow broad to little more than a puddle, the firm fitted up the wherry *Caroline* as a kind of suction dredger. A large steam engine driving a centrifugal pump was fitted in the hold, the idea being that the weed should be sucked from the broad and deposited, by way of a floating pipeline, on the marshes. The *Caroline* saw little or no service in this guise, however.

J. S. Hobrough made a habit of buying up old wherries as they became redundant for cargo carrying and employed them in his business. The firm was engaged in a good deal of lightering work, at one time transporting between 1,000 and 1,600 tons of coal a week from Trowse railway sidings to the gas and electricity works in the city of Norwich, but in later days the wherries were used mainly in connection with dredging.

When they were too far gone to be of any further use afloat the wherries were sunk along the banks of the Yare to help keep the bank in good shape, and some were sunk on Surlingham Broad with the intention of forming a deep channel across the broad.

When J. S. Hobrough retired in 1940 at the age of 75 the firm was sold to May Gurney & Co. Ltd. of Trowse, who continued to use the dockyard at Thorpe St. Andrew as a base for dredging operations on the local rivers. Around 1950 they were still operating the wherries *Dora, Maud, Bell, Malve* (formerly the *Olga*), *Shamrock, Elder* (formerly the *Iolanthe*), *Primus, Secunda, Dispatch,* and *Go Forward* and the iron wherries *Crystal, Uranus* and *Diamond*.

Sunk in the dykes near the dockyard at this period was an assortment of old craft including the wherries *Macadam* (originally *Unknown*), *Jessie, Caroline, Stalham Trader* and *John Henry,* which were eventually destroyed as the dykes were filled with tons of spoil from the holds of wherries working with the dredgers on the Norwich River.

Several of these wherries were fitted with motors, mainly small Thornycroft petrol-paraffin engines. A few steam wherries had been built during the second half of the nineteenth century, and the first internal combustion motors were introduced about 1915 in an attempt to compete with big steel lighters of the kind brought on to the river a few years earlier by Henry Newhouse's Yare and Waveney Lighter Company. With a capacity of about 100 tons, these were towed by steam lighters such as the

The wherry *Caroline* fitted up as a suction dredger in the 1930s.

The *Elder*, one of the wherries used in connection with dredging operations on the Yare in the 1950s, was built at Bungay as the *Iolanthe* for W.D. & A.E. Walker. She is seen here soon after her launching in 1892.

Opal and *Topaz* or by small steam tugs. The *Topaz* served for many years as a dumb lighter after her engines had been removed.

One of the first wherries to be converted was the *Bell*, which had a two-cylinder petrol-paraffin engine fitted about 1915. Bought by James Hobrough & Son about three years later, she was hauled out and strengthened and had her engine replaced by a 20hp. single-cylinder Kromhout crude oil engine, which gave her enough power to tow two wherries when trading between Yarmouth and Norwich. As the engine was fitted in the cabin at the stern a new cabin was built into the forepeak to provide accommodation for the crew.

Barclay Pallett's *Ella* and Thain's *Lord Roberts* were both fitted with Thornycroft $7\frac{1}{2}$hp. petrol-paraffin engines in 1930, and Hobrough's *Wanderer* and Rolfe's *Primus* were motorised shortly after.

But this was no more than a last-ditch defence; the day of the wherry was all but past. With the building of the new electricity power station near Trowse Eye in the 1920s coal was brought direct to the site by motor coasters operated by F. T. Everard

& Sons Ltd., and the same type of small steam and motor coaster brought other cargoes up to the city as the maritime trade of the Yare experienced a revival undreamt of since the 1830s. It was, though, road transport which really killed the wherry traffic, and by 1949 there was not a single sailing wherry trading on the Broads.

Apart from the few wherries still employed by May Gurney there was only a handful of motor wherries at work, including the *Ella,* then owned by Nat Bircham, and the *Lord Roberts, Fir* (formerly *Crowhurst*) and *I'll Try,* all owned by members of the Thain family.

It was at this juncture that a number of enthusiasts hit on the idea of forming an organisation to preserve at least one trading wherry under sail. The Norfolk Wherry Trust was formed following a meeting in the Stuart Hall, Norwich, on February 23, 1949, at which Mr. Humphrey Boardman put the proposition that "this meeting agrees to the formation of the Norfolk Wherry Trust in order to preserve, in perpetuity, one or more examples of the Norfolk trading wherry."

The wherry *Plane,* formerly the *Albion,* was made available by Colman's, who had used her for some years for lightering within their works at Carrow, and after a four-month refit at the Yarmouth shipyard of Fellows & Co. Ltd., during which she was docked in one of the nineteenth-century timber-built dry docks there, she was ready for her new job. While she was refitting a new mast and gaff had to be made for her and a new sail was made in the Lowestoft sail loft of Jeckells & Son Ltd.

The Mayor of Yarmouth was aboard her when she made her first trip upriver under her new owners in October, 1949, recalling the days of Burgh Water Frolic. And the Lord Mayor of Norwich welcomed her at Hardley Cross, the limit of Norwich Corporation's jurisdiction over the Yare, reviving memories of the ancient ceremony in which the Mayors of Yarmouth and Norwich once met there annually in the course of an inspection of their respective boundaries.

Soon the *Albion,* given back her old name, was carrying sugar beet to the British Sugar Corporation factory at Cantley and taking timber from Yarmouth to Norwich occasionally for one of the city's timber firms as well as carrying other cargoes about the Norfolk rivers. Early in 1950 she loaded a cargo of building materials in Norwich for the repair of the *Berney Arms,* once a wherrymen's pub and almost cut off from the outside world except by water.

At one time the Wherry Trust had hoped it might be possible to keep the *Albion* trading. But in 1952 the Trust made a heavy loss and the hopes of members turned to disappointment. At the Annual meeting the next year it was decided that the *Albion* should cease regular full-time trading and should instead be let to parties of Scouts and other young people during the summer months.

She was not, however, converted into a pleasure wherry. The youngsters had to rough it on hammocks slung in the hold in much the same way that some of the hardy early visitors to the Broads had done a century or so before. And she continued to carry sugar beet to Cantley each autumn, until the British Sugar Corporation decided it was inconvenient to accept some beet by one means and some by another and confined itself entirely to road transport.

Even so, all was still not plain sailing for the Wherry Trust. When racing on Breydon in 1952 the *Albion* broke her mast and the Trust had to pay £180 for another to be made, and in November, 1957, she sank at Hardley Staithe, on the Yare not very far from Loddon, while loaded with 40 tons of sugar beet. Though she was not seriously damaged by this misadventure, the sinking showed that work needed to be done; after all, she was almost sixty years old.

She again sank just over two years later, this time at Berney Arms, and had to have repairs at Richards Ironworks at Lowestoft. That mishap cost the Wherry Trust around £1,000, and, although the insurers eventually provided £600 towards that, it became clear that the Trust was going to have to find more support if it was to carry on.

The Duke of Edinburgh offered his support as patron when the Wherry Trust held a "Save the Wherry Week" in 1966 with the object of raising £2,000 to refit the *Albion* over a three-year period. Businessmen in Norfolk and in other parts of the country came to the Trust's assistance; in 1968 the *Albion* received a new mast made in a Potter Heigham boatyard as a gift, and a new sail was paid for by a Broads yacht hiring agency as a contribution to the Trust's efforts.

In spite of all difficulties the Norfolk Wherry Trust has kept the *Albion* sailing, and there is every hope that she will survive long enough for the Trust members to celebrate her centenary in 1998.

Traditional materials are increasingly difficult to come by, and in the winter of 1985-86 Trust members used a piece of Australian jarrah wood given by Darby Brothers, the Beccles timber merchants, to make a new main beam for the *Albion*. By using up-to-date methods of timber preservation and by taking care always to keep her in first-class repair the Trust continues to carry out the intentions of its founders, to give holidaymakers a chance to see an example of a trading wherry under sail.

In the early days of the Wherry Trust there had been ambitious plans to build a new wherry, and later there was talk of repairing the *Lord Roberts*, which had been given to the Trust when she became unfit for further work. More recently it has been proposed that the *Lord Roberts* should become a static exhibit at a Broadland museum; one can only hope that this project will meet with better success than the unhappy attempt to restore the *Olga* as an exhibit for the Maritime Museum for East Anglia at Yarmouth.

If such a museum is eventually opened the *Lord Roberts* might well find herself alongside the last of the keels, which was in 1985 raised by a team of divers under Theo Douglas-Sherwood from her resting place beside the Yare, taken up to Norwich and lifted from the water so that preservation work could begin. The keel will certainly never again set sail, but given the will and the necessary money she could one day form an impressive museum exhibit.

The corporate efforts of the Wherry Trust are being matched by a few private individuals such as Essex millwright Vincent Pargeter and his wife Linda, who are rebuilding the *Maud*, which had been sunk on Ranworth Broad with the *Bell* when May Gurney replaced their ageing wherries with steel lighters. Reconstruction of the *Maud* will be a long-term project carried through by Linda and Vincent in their own spare time, for the cost of having the work done professionally would be far beyond their means.

Another enthusiast is Peter Bower, who acquired the wherry yacht *Olive* in 1974 and has since been operating her in the traditional way taking parties of holidaymakers for cruises on the Broads. The *Olive* was built by Ernest Collins at Wroxham in 1909 and remained in their hire fleet for some half a century; to celebrate her seventy-fifth birthday Peter staged an exhibition on board and toured the rivers, opening the exhibition wherever the *Olive* found a mooring.

In her seventy-fifth year the *Olive* sailed on Oulton Broad in company with the pleasure wherry *Solace*, the only survivor under sail of her kind, and the wherry yacht *Lady Edith*, formerly the *Norada*, which like the *Olive* is operating as a charter vessel. It was a spectacle from the past.

Long may the *Albion*, the *Solace*, the *Olive* and the *Lady Edith* sail on; and may the day not be far off when they will be joined by the *Maud* and possibly even by other restored craft of a bygone age.

A number of old wherries were sunk in dykes at Thorpe St Andrew. This one, the *John Henry*, was burnt when the dyke was filled with dredging spoil about 1948.

One sole survivor, the *Albion*, still sails on thanks to the efforts of the Norfolk Wherry Trust. *Albion's* future lies with the degree of public support, in terms of such things as membership, finance and materials, given to the Trust.

APPENDIX ONE

Equipment of a Wherry

The equipment of a wherry included:

A pump.

Two quants (22' or 24').

A boathook (19')

Two rond anchors.

A dropping chain.

A rag mop.

Two fenders made of bass with cork filling.

A light towline 100' in length.

Plankhooks on wherries carrying timber. They were used for pulling the deals into position in the hold.

Two long deals. They were placed from the wherry to the bank in order to load or unload the wherry with barrows. (22' x 11" x 3")

Two quarter deals (16' x 11" x 3"). These deals were long enough to stretch across the hold.

"Right-up" irons (2 sizes). These irons hooked on the inside of the hold and one end of the quarter deal rested on it. This end was lower in the hold than the other end which rested on the top of the rightups. When the barrow was placed on the lower end of the quarter deal it did not need so much effort in filling it from the bottom of the hold.

Two barrows of special design with no legs.

"Bass" (coir) mooring ropes.

A stone water bottle.

A lantern. This was never used, wherrymen said they could see better without it as it blinded them.

Lines of Wherry *Albion*

Reproduced by kind permission of Henry Higgs, naval architect and surveyor, London.

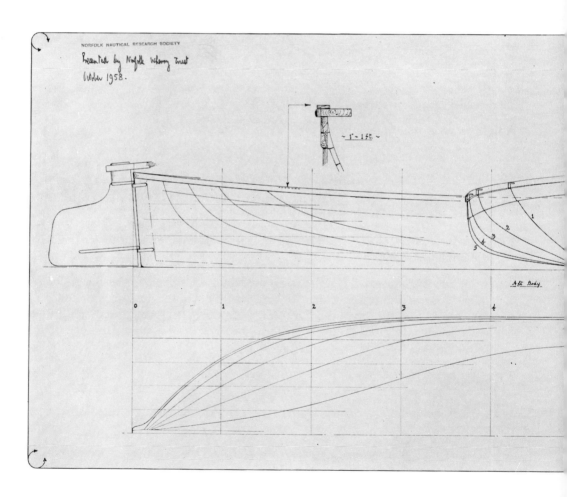

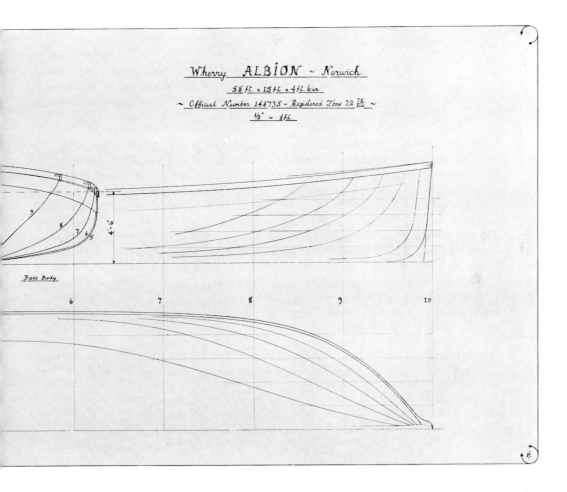

Wherry ALBION ~ Norwich
58 ft. × 15 ft. × 4 ft. 6 in.
~ Official Number 148735 ~ Registered Tons 22 $\frac{78}{100}$ ~
½" ~ 1 ft.

Fore Body

The River Reaches

WHERRYMEN had their own names for the waterways, as has been mentioned briefly in Chapter 1. The Yare below Breydon was at Yarmouth just "The River", while higher up it was referred to as "The Yarmouth River". Above Breydon it was "The Norwich River". The Bure was "The North River" and the Waveney "The Beccles River".

Even the early mapmakers and historians were not very sure of themselves when dealing with the rivers. The Yare and the Waveney were not easy to confuse, even if the Yare was awkward enough to turn aside and circumvent the city of Norwich, leaving it to the Wensum to bear the city's merchandise for the last mile or so, but the northern rivers were such as to muddle them thoroughly.

Swinden in his *History of Yarmouth*, published in 1772, quotes the earlier historian Manship as saying "the third called Thurn (or Bure) which first ariseth near Holt ... and so ... to Yarmouth aforesaid". Here Thurne applies to the whole length of the Bure and not to the stream to which later maps applied the name Thurne.

In the middle of the nineteenth century the Ordnance Survey maps dropped the name Thurne altogether as far as the waterways are concerned and called the tributary, from its confluence with the Bure towards Martham Broad, "The Hundred Stream", obviously because that waterway provided a boundary between the Hundreds of West Flegg and Happing.

Looking at a map, one sees that the boundary does not in fact follow the stream quite down to Thurne Mouth but leaves it about a mile above the point at which the waters of the tributary mingle with those of the Bure, striking off to the westward along the line of the Hundred Dyke. It may well be that this dyke represents an earlier course of the River Ant, just as the Fleet Dyke leading to South Walsham Broad is part of an old channel of the Bure, marked as "Old River" on Faden's map of Norfolk in 1797.

Modern maps apply the name Thurne to that length of the stream between the Bure and Kendal Dyke, the section above that being termed "The Hundred River".

In the days of sail every alteration of direction, however slight, called for action on the part of the wherryman. The slightest bend in the river meant that the sail had to be trimmed; or perhaps it would bring the wind almost dead ahead and force the wherryman to put his vessel about, to tack through the next reach in a series of short boards.

A reach is, as any wherryman would tell you, "just that much clear water as you can see ahead after making a turn." The banks, usually reed-fringed, cut out much of the view on either side and a bend which is hardly noticeable on the map is quite sufficient to put an end to a reach. Few of the reaches on the Norfolk and Suffolk rivers are more than half a mile long, and many are much less.

Each reach had its name, though few of the names used by the wherrymen found their way on to maps. A. J. Rudd in his *Illustrated Guide to Fishing in Norfolk Waters* recorded many of the reaches, and C. R. Hamilton did the same on his well-known charts of the Broadland rivers, while others have compiled lists containing at least some of the names. Several writers have attempted to explain a few of the more curious names, some producing more plausible explanations than others.

Generally speaking, the names of the reaches were derived either from some feature of nearby scenery, perhaps an alder carr, a distinctive building or a drainage mill, or from the name of an owner or occupier of land in the vicinity.

Examples of reaches given a personal name are Bachelor's River Reach and Bachelor's Boathouse Reach on the Bure above Coltishall; the Batchelor family had an estate at Horstead in the eighteenth century. Just below these reaches is Largate Reach, which got its name from the ancient name of a district extending to the river north-west of Horstead Church.

Hagen's Folly Reach between Belaugh and Wroxham referred to an unsuccessful marl pit opened by a man named Hagen, while Cinder Ovens Reach at Horning, or Cinderobin as it was called by one old wherryman, took its name from the kilns in which coal dust, the sweepings of colliers' holds brought up from Yarmouth by wherry, was coked for use in the malthouses on Horning quay.

A difficulty about recording these reaches is that the names are subject to considerable change over the course of years. Some names have been corrupted or have lost their original meaning, while in some cases old names have given way to new. Especially is this true of those called after a person living in a riverside house or the owner of a drainage mill, which would almost invariably take the name of a new occupier.

Sometimes pronunciation, tradition and supposition have clouded the origin of a name. Take, for example, the reach below Ranner Dam, or Ranworth Dam as it should perhaps be written; the name is given variously as Beggar's Hope, Beggar's Oak, Bagger's Oak and Badger's Holt Reach. The hillside to the north may well have been the haunt of badgers when these animals were still to be found in this part of Norfolk, but on the other hand A. J. Rudd, giving the name as Beggar's Oak Reach, explains that it was so called "from a tramp having hung himself on an oak tree in this reach. The oak, like the beggar, is now defunct". Beggar's Oaks and Beggar's Bushes with similar stories linked with them are not unknown elsewhere.

The long straight stretch of the Bure between the mouth of the Ant and the abbey of St. Benet's is known as The Ward, and it has been suggested that it gained this title because when the cut was made, probably some time in the eighteenth century, the marsh so cut off was "awarded" to Horning parish; this marsh is known as Ward Marsh. A more likely derivation is from the family name of Ward, as members of this family had land at South Walsham and in neighbouring parishes in the 1700s.

Lower down, Mautby Swim and Runham Swim were so called from the practice of swimming cattle across the river to and from the marshes. It was usual to carry the leader of the herd over in a ferry boat; the remainder of the herd were then easily persuaded to swim across to rejoin their leader. Walter Rye said in *A Month on the Norfolk Broads* that he had refused to believe this explanation of the name until one autumn he saw "seven or eight leisurely walk in, and in the most clumsy fashion, it must be said, get to the other bank."

Some of the most expressive names are to be found in the lower reaches of the Bure. Muckhole Reach, otherwise known as Spicey Island, ran alongside the Corporation refuse tip; what had earlier been known as Mouth of North End became after the building of the Norwich and Yarmouth railway in 1844 Terminus Reach or Old Rail; and Bowling Green Reach took its name from the bowling green attached to a once well-known tavern.

Some reaches gained their names in a thoroughly down-to-earth fashion; Train Reach on the Norwich River at Strumpshaw was so called because wherrymen sailing that stretch had a good view of the Norwich-Yarmouth railway line, which there runs parallel with the river. There was an element of humour in the naming of others; Turn Pudden Reach or Hole, immediately below the Hagen's Folly Reach already mentioned, is said to have got its name from the habit of wherrymen of nipping below to turn the pudding on the stove when they reached this point.

The following lists have been compiled from various lists, mostly those collected by Mr. Horace Bolingbroke, and are as complete as possible. An attempt has been made to relate the reaches to various riverside landmarks in order to assist the reader: the positions of these may in some cases be only approximate, as it is impossible in such a list to indicate whether they lie at the beginning or towards the end of a reach, and only in a few cases do they mark the dividing point between one reach and another. Such landmarks are in bold type.

RIVER BURE

Yarmouth to Aylsham

Bowling Green Reach, Yarmouth
Mouth of North End, Terminus Reach or
    Old Rail
Crowe's Quay or North Quay
Sluice Reach
Muckhole Reach or Spicey Island Reach
Cinder Oven or East-and-West Reach
Black House Reach
One Mile House Reach
Two Mile Steam Mill
Black Mill
Frogs Hall Reach
Three Mile House Reach
Scaregap
No Man's Friend
Four Mile Short Reach
Four Mile Long Reach
Dry Reach
Five Mile Long Reach
Mautby Swim
Bowling Alley or Six Mile Reach
Five Mile House
Runham Swim
Howes' Short Reach
Martha's Reach
Building New Staithe Reach
Duffus (Dovehouse) Reach
Strutt's Haven or Sluts Haven
Stracey Arms public house
Seven Mile House Reach
Black Mill Reach
Tunstall Mill Reach
Tunstall Dyke
Tunstall Dyke Reach
Stokesby Short Reaches
Stokesby
Stokesby Ferry Reach
Trett's Mill Reach
Two Mills Reach
Muck Fleet
Muckfleet Reach
Horseshoe Reach
Acle Dyke
Hermitage
Acle Bridge Reach

Acle Bridge
Acle Bridge Reach
Fishley Mill Reach
Lower Davy's Mill Reach
Upton Dyke
Upper Davy's Mill Reach
Oby Short Reach
Thurne Reach or Long Thurne
Thurne Mouth
Mile Bars
South Walsham Southerly Reach
St. Benet's Abbey
St. Benet's Reach
Fleet Dyke
South Walsham Dyke Reach
Ward Reach
Ant Mouth
Jay's Short Reach or Horning Old Hall
    Reach
Badger's Holt, Badger's Oak, Beggar's Oak
    or Bagger's Oak Reach
Dyke to Malthouse Broad
Ranner (Ranworth) Dam
Old Staithe Reach
Horning Church Short Reach
Horning Church Long Reach
Cockshoot Dyke Reach
Ferry Reach
Horning Ferry
Ferry Mill Reach
Horning Town Reach
Cinder Oven Reach
Hoveton or Horning Long Reach
**Parsons Dyke leads to Woodbastwick
    Decoy Broad**
Dydles
Decoy Staithe Reach
Blackcurrant Carr
The Dam leads to Hoveton Great Broad
Fox Burrows
Salhouse Broad Reach
**Gravel Dyke leads to Hoveton Great
    Broad**
Old Woman's Pulk
Easterly Reach

157

RIVER BURE continued

Dirty River Reach
Willow Trees Reach
Hill Piece
Snipe's Water Reach
Dairy House or Skeleton House Reach
Clark's Reach
Bridge Reach
Wroxham Bridge
Mill Carr
Turn Pudden Hole
Hagen's Folly Reach
Cockle Fen Dyke
Two Acre or Twelve Acre Reach
Belaugh Mill Reach
Bone Yard Reach
Wroxham Town Reach
Priest's Reach
Belaugh Broad Reach
Avenue Reach
Sheepwash Reach
Becksmouth
Marl Staithe
Doctor's Cut
Belaugh River
Belaugh Church
Belaugh Shoals
Belaugh Carr or Cook's Carr
Little Duffus (Dovehouse) Reach
Horstead Heath Reach or Long Strip
Coltshed Reaches
Allen's boatyard
Boatwright's Reaches
Anchor Reach
Common Reach or Coltishall Hall Reach
Manor House Reach
Osier Carr
White's Reach or Kemp's Reach
Lock Cut
Coltishall Lock
Bridge Reach
Coltishall Bridge
Bream Corner
Horstead Shoals
Ives' Cut
Largate Reach
Alder Carr
Bachelor's or Besseter's River

Bachelor's Boathouse Reach
Sallow Bush
New Cut
Boathouse Carr
Mayton Bridge
Mayton Bridge Reach
Goose Turd Hill or Ladbrooke's Reach
Buxton Long Reach
Railway bridge
Buxton Mill Reach
Buxton Mill and Lock
Bream Corner
Tanner's Reach
Ram's Row Reach
Lamas Hall Reach
Smith's Holes
Harris Planting (plantation) Reach
Blake's Alder Carr
Ladies' Bower
King's Beck
New Cut
Alder Carr
Long Planting (plantation)
Park Bridge
Oxnead Lock Cut
Oxnead Lock
Oxnead Bridge Reach
Common Reach
Lime Kiln Reach
Burgh Lock
Burgh Lock Cut
Burgh Mill
Burgh Mill Reach
Sayer's Ham
Cradle Bridge
Cradle Bridge Reach
Burgh Bridge
County Bridge Reach
Thirty Kep Carr
Case's Ham
Wolsey's Bridge
Aylsham Lock Cut
Aylsham Lock
Aylsham Lock Reach
Oak Corner or Royal Oak Reach
Aylsham Basin

RIVER ANT
Ant Mouth to Antingham

Mouth of the Ant
Dykes Mouth
Mill Brig or Little Duffus Reach
Jay's Mill Reach
Mussel Corner
Wright's Mill Reach
Ludham Bridge
Horseshoe Reach
Old Neave's Reach
Neave's Mill
Horning Fen
Pestle's or Spuntney's Mill Reach
Red House Reach
Baldwin's Mill Reach
Narrow Strip
Howe Hill Reach
Howe Hill Mill Reach
Clay Rack
Catfield Old Staithe Reach
Skeleton Reach
Mud Half-mile
Irstead Shoals
Icehouse Reach
Cox's Eel Sett
Barton Broad
Paddy's Lane
Barton Bank
Willow Tree

Shukfer's Eel Sett
Mouth of Stalham Broad (navigable to
  Stalham and Sutton staithes)
Hunn's sett
New Cut
Prones Dyke
Durrel's Mill
Smallburgh Fen
Wayford Bridge
Tunnage Long Reach
Tunbridge or Tonnage Bridge
Narrow Guts
Ruston Common
Bushes Marsh
St. Villiers
Honing Lock
Honing Bridge
Taylor's Plantation
Briggate Lock and Bridge
Pustle's Cut
Ebridge Lock and Mill
Bacton Wood Staithe, Bridge and Lock
Roiston (Austin) Bridge
Swafield Staithe and Bridge
Bradfield Two Locks
Bradfield Broad and Bridge
Antingham Bone Mill
Antingham Basin

RIVER THURNE
Thurne Mouth to Somerton

Thurne Mouth
Short Thurne
Thurne Dyke
Coldharbour
Ludham Dyke Reach
Oules' Reach
Repps Dyke Reach
Skeleton or Johnson's Reach
Heigham Bridge Reach
Potter Heigham Bridge
Bridge Reach

Half-mile Rail or Shannon Wall
Grapes' Mill
Martham Steam Mill Reach
Kendal Dyke
Martham Ferry Reach
Martham Ferry
Martham River
Dungeon Corner
Somerton Broad (marked on maps as
  Martham Broad)
Somerton Dyke

THE NORWICH RIVER

Breydon
Burgh Flats
Berney Arms Reach
Five Mile House Reach
Tilekiln Reach
Six Mile Rond Reach
Six Mile House Reach
Seven Mile House Reach
The Bowling Alley
Eight Mile Trees Reach
Railway Swing Bridge
Reedham Town Reach
Taylor's Reach
Reedham Ferry
Reedham Ferry Reach
Hardley Cross
Cross Reach
Norton Staithe
Little Head Reach
Hardley Dyke
Hardley Reach or Dirty Hole Reach
Devil's House Reach
Limpenhoe Reach
Cantley Red House
Cantley Reach
Under Langley
Langley Dyke
Langley Lower Short Reach
Langley Middle Short Reach
Langley Upper Short Reach
Hassingham Dyke Reach
Langley Steam Mill
Hassingham Hoves
Buckenham Reach
Buckenham Ferry
Buckenham Ferry Reach
Buckenham Horseshoes Reach
Ashentree Reach
Rockland Reach

Rockland Dyke Reach
The Train or Train Reach
Coldham Hall
Coldham Hall Reach
Brundall Short Reach
Brundall Long Reach
Back of the Fen or Grease House Reach
Surlingham Ferry
Surlingham Ferry Reach
Horseshoe Reach
Surlingham Brickyard Reach, Brick Kiln Reach or Six Mile Staithe Reach
Jimmy Norton's or Underhill's Reach
Bramerton Woods End Reach
Woods End public house
Postwick Reach
Postwick Grove Reach
Thorpe Short Reach
Hobrough's Dock
Whitlingham Reach
Cave Reach
The Cut and Thorpe Broad
Alder Carr
Trowse Eye
Swing Bridge Reach
Carrow Bridge Reach
Carrow Bridge (The old bridge was some distance below the present one)
King Street Reach
Foundry Bridge
Ferry Reach
Bishop's Bridge
Bishop's Bridge Reach
Cow Tower
Hospital Reach
Dead Walls
Whitefriars Bridge
Quayside

RIVER WAVENEY
Yarmouth to Bungay

Burgh Flats
Belton Short Reach
Dolers Reach
Bowling Alley or Belton Long Reach
Seven Mile House Reach
Humberley Reach or Going round
    Humberley
St. Olaves Reach
St. Olaves Bridge
Herringfleet Bridge Reach
Herringfleet railway bridge
Hole o' the Hill Reach
St. Thomas's Reach or Long Tom
Somerleyton Brickworks
Somerleyton Railway Bridge
Somerleyton Bridge Reach
Steam Mill or Barber's Pole Reach
White House Reach
White House Dyke
Long Galley Reach
Short Galley Reach
Carvers Corner
Oulton Dyke Reach
Oulton Dyke
Burgh Staithe Reach
Burgh St. Peter Staithe
Carlton Mill Reach
Share Mill
Eight Mile Trees Reach
Seven Mile Carr Reach
Seven Mile Carr Lower Short Reach
Cove Short Reach
Six Mile Corner

Cove Long Reach
Worlingham Mill Reach or Hannah's Yard
    Reach
Worlingham Mill
Four Mile Dam Reach
Three Mile Mill Reach
Stanley Bridge Reach
Aldeby railway bridge
Stanley Carr Reach
Wherry Dyke
Boaters or Boat'us Hill Reach
Middle Mile Reach
Upper Reach
Beccles Sluice Reach
Beccles Bridge
Beccles Town Reach
The Narrows
Northerly Reach
Nine Tree Reach
Dunburgh Hill Reach
Geldeston Dyke
Geldeston Dyke Reach
Easterly or Barsham Reach
Shipmeadow (or Geldeston) Lock
Lock Reach
Roast Beef Corner Reach
Shipmeadow Shoals Reach
Roundabouts Reach
Old Moll's Lock Reach
Ellingham Lock
Wainford Lock
The Mile
Bungay Staithe

APPENDIX FOUR

Advertised for Sale

ADVERTISEMENTS for the sale of vessels which appear in local newspapers from time to time naturally tell us quite a lot about the craft concerned, and often they tell us something about the circumstances in which they came to be sold. Sometimes they came on the market because of the death of the owner, sometimes because of his failure in business.

In the *Norwich Mercury* of February 27th, 1779, there appeared the following:

To be sold by auction. On Monday the first of March next ensuing, unless sooner disposed of by private contract.

The keel or vessel called the Hand and Hand, burthen 50 tons, now lying at Norwich. For particulars enquire of Mr. Wymer, Attorney, or Mr. Long, grocer, at Norwich, Assignee of the estate and effects of Joseph Taylor, the Younger, of the City of Norwich, keelman.

Some of the craft that came on the market were brand new. Within weeks of the Hand and Hand being advertised there appeared an advertisement, in the *Norwich Mercury* of March 13th, for a wherry:

YARMOUTH To be sold in the Yard of the late Peter Kirkman, a large new built Wherry, built with English Oak Board, which will be finished in about ten or 12 days. Any Person that have a mind to treat about the said Boat by applying to the Widow Kirkman, may be answered. She is 51 feet long and 13 wide, supposing to carry 20 Chaldron of coals.

Then on October 23rd of the same year there appeared in both the *Norwich Mercury* and the *Norfolk Chronicle* an advertisement for a "hatch keel."

A hatch keel to be sold at Coltishall, Norfolk, called the John and Joseph, burthen about 50 tons, and all the materials belonging to her. N.B. The keel has lately undergone a thorough repair. For further particulars enquire of John Fiddy, or Joseph Browne, of Coltishall aforesaid.

The researcher wishes he could indeed enquire for further details of this interesting craft.

The *Mercury* of March 9th, 1805, contained a "for sale" notice which is of interest:

On Monday, March 11, 1805, at Four o'clock in the Afternoon, at Mr. Jacob Wright's, Carrow Abbey, Norwich.

The Wherry, called the Betsy, of Beccles, burthen 18 chaldrons, built 4 years, in good repair, with new sail.

The *Ipswich Journal* of June 10th, 1815, advertised the sale on June 21st "by order of the trustees of John Baltis, ship builder, all that commodious and well situated

Dock Yard in South Town otherwise Little Yarmouth, near Cobholm Island, lately occupied by Mr. Thomas Douglas, ship builder, together with a dwelling house, two workshops, steam copper, sawpit." The following day all the "household furniture and stock in trade of the said John Baltis with a wherry of above 25 chaldron, nearly half built", was to be sold.

In the same newspaper of June 5th, 1824, there appeared an advertisement for a wherry of more mature years.

To Merchants, Watermen, and Others. Wherry Three Brothers, 18 tons burden, to be sold on 19 June 1824 on the Quay, Yarmouth. John Thurtell, Jun., strongly recommends the above Craft to the attention of Merchants and others, as she is in excellent repair, her Mainsail and Bonnet quite new, and well found in stores of every description. She is now hauled up for inspection, at MR. JONES'S (Boat Builder) WHARF, Beccles, where she will remain until a few days of the Sale, on which day she can be inspected at Yarmouth Bridge.

The following year, on April 30th, the *Norwich Mercury* carried a more concise advertisement.

To be sold. A wherry, called the Escape, burthen 21 chaldron,—apply to James Cozens and Son, Merchants, St. Benedict's Street, Norwich.

One might think from such advertisements that these wherries carried nothing but coal. An advertisement in the *Norwich Mercury* of February 25th, 1837, shows us that this is far from a true picture.

Wherry for Sale. All that nearly new and well-built WHERRY or MARKET BOAT, Mayflower, of Palling, of about 14 Chaldron Coals and 9½ last barley burthen, with all her excellent Stores, Barrows, Planks, & c. for the trade.

The Wherry will be lying for inspection at the Bridge Quay, Yarmouth, from the 1st March to the Morning of Sale.

Just what her stores consisted of is not recorded, but the *Norfolk Chronicle* of September 21st, 1850, was more forthcoming in this respect.

To be sold by auction by Pettingill on Wednesday 25 September 1850 on the quay near the foot of the bridge, Yarmouth, by order of the mortgagee.

The wherry William and Elizabeth, burthen 37 tons, built in Norwich 1842.

Inventory. Mast with about 35 cwt of lead at the heel. Capital rigging, new sail, two anchors, two mooring ropes, warp chain, dredge, two shovels, three claws, boat hook, two tar buckets, etc., etc. The wherry will be laying at the quay near the bridge for three days previous to the sale and may be inspected with her stores by application on board.

Finally a notice from the *Norwich Mercury* of March 22nd, 1851:

Fras. Clowes is favoured with Instructions from the Proprietor, to sell by auction at Rudrum's Wharf, King Street, Norwich, on Friday next, the 28th day of March, 1851, at 11 o'clock precisely, in separate lots, those two fast and favourite wherries, the Snipe, 28 tons burden, and the Lapwing, 34 tons burden, with all their masts, sails, patent winches, tarpawlings, anchors, quants, chain-hooks, purchase-gears, chain runners, and other necessary stores. The former of these Wherries was thoroughly repaired last October, and on the latter a large sum of money was expended in rebuilding her a few years since, and as the proprietor wholly declines the water carrying business, his instructions are to sell without reserve.

Also a very excellent Wherry's Sail. For further particulars apply to the Auctioneer, St. Andrews Hall Plain, Norwich.

APPENDIX FIVE

Brown Boats, White Boats and Punts

The lateeners were not, of course, the only strictly local type of yacht to be developed on the Broads, where natural conditions imposed their own mould on the craft turned out by local boatbuilders. However, a history of Broads yachts would need a book to itself, and the story of the later racing craft cannot be adequately told here. Nor can the story of the sailing clubs that sired the various one-design classes be told in so small a space.

One of the most successful of the local racing classes is the Broads One-Design, which came from the drawing board of a famous yacht designer, Linton Hope, at the turn of the century. The Brown Boats, as they are always known, have proved as successful at sea off Lowestoft as on the inland waters for which they were built, and their varnished hulls with spoon bows are still familiar on their home waters.

Some members of the class have, however, strayed far from the Broads. In 1956 *Garganey* (No. 24) and *Avocet* (No. 11) sailed across the English Channel and back, and at some time *Dotterel* (No. 8) was taken by her owner to the West Indies, where he sailed her in very different waters. In the class's diamond jubilee year, 1960, only *Dotterel* and *Turnstone* (No. 15) were missing from the class register, which then contained thirty-one names.

The success of the brown boats having been noticed by local yachtsmen, the Yare and Bure Sailing Club, one of the clubs which thirty years later amalgamated to form the Norfolk Broads Yacht Club, decided in 1908 to ask several local designers to submit drawings for a one-design class. A design by a young Cantley boatbuilder, Ernest Woods, was chosen, and Woods was given the task of building the first eight boats. He built every succeeding member of the class, and in the year of the class's golden jubilee he was working on the 67th.

These gunter-rigged half-deckers were justifiably popular, for they were among the few racing yachts which had no vices and were as useful for day cruising and for general pleasure sailing as they were for racing. The Yare and Bure O.D.s, or White Boats as they were soon familiarly known to Broads yachtsmen, have kept up the tradition of butterfly names for more than half a century, though a few moths have crept in from time to time and No. 67 was named *Golden Jubilee* on completion in 1958.

A rather similar half-decker, the Waveney O.D., was designed in 1928 by W. S. Parker, the Lowestoft boatbuilder and designer.

Perhaps the most distinctive of all the Broads racing craft are the punts, developed from the gunpunts used by the wildfowlers of old. There are many different types of gunpunt, though all share a shallow draught and the ability to mount an enormous muzzle-loading gun which could slaughter a whole flock of birds at a single discharge. The type in use on the northern broads was in many respects more shapely than the variety employed by some coastal wildfowlers, and it was not unknown for these craft to carry sail.

Some 14-18 foot in length, these low double-ended craft were partly decked, leaving a long cockpit amidships in which the fowler could lie flat when approaching fowl. The old-time marshmen doubtless had their fun at water frolics in these workaday craft, but they would probably be startled to see the racing punts which have now developed from them.

When the Norfolk Punt Club was founded in 1926 the rules were aimed at keeping the punt a craft which could be sculled to fowl, but the modern punt is a high-performance racing machine with bermudian sail and centreboard.

A Select Bibliography

A GREAT number of books have been written about the Broads, most of these books dealing with the scenery of the region and with yachting cruises on the rivers. For an almost complete list of those published up to 1921 see *Books on the Broads, A Chronological Bibliography,* compiled by George Stephen, issued by Norwich City Library in 1921. Those listed below are of particular interest as dealing with the waterways and those who sailed on them in more detail than most or else are the most important general books on this specialised region.

The waterways, etc.

Stark and Robberds. *Scenery of the Rivers of Norfolk, from pictures painted by James Stark, with historical and geological descriptions by J. W. Robberds, Jun. Esq.* 1834.

W. A. Dutt and others. *The Norfolk Broads,* 1903 (and later editions).

E. A. Ellis. *The Broads,* Collins 1965.

J. M. Lambert, J. N. Jennings, C. T. Smith, Charles Green and J. N. Hutchinson. *The making of the Broads: a reconsideration of their origin in the light of new evidence.* R. G. S. Research Memoir No. 3, 1960.

J. N. Jennings. *The Origin of the Broads.* R.G.S. Research Series No. 2, 1952.

Social history, etc.

P. H. Emerson and T. F. Goodall. *Life and Landscape on the Norfolk Broads,* 1886.

P. H. Emerson. *A Son of the Fens,* 1892.

Arthur Patterson. *Man and Nature on Tidal Waters,* 1909.

Arthur Patterson. *Wild-fowlers and Poachers,* 1929.

Other books by Arthur Patterson also contain interesting references to the watermen and wild-fowlers who inhabited the area, though dealing mainly with wild life.

Wherries

Roy Clark. *Black-Sailed Traders.* Putnam, 1961.

G. Colman Green. *The Norfolk Wherry,* 1937.

Norfolk Wherry Trust. *The Norfolk Wherry,* 1952.

Yachting

Nicholas Everitt. *Broadland Sport,* 1902.

Oliver Ready. *Life and Sport on the Norfolk Broads,* 1910. (Republished in abridged form as *Countryman on the Broads,* MacGibbon and Kee, 1967.)

Pleasure wherry cruises

Blue Peter. *A Week in a Wherry on the Norfolk Broads,* 1890.

Librairie Delagrave (publisher). *En Wherry: Trois semaines dans les Broads du Norfolk,* 1892.

H. M. Doughty. *Summer in Broadland: gipsying in East Anglian waters,* 1889.

H. M. Doughty. *Friesland Meres and through the Netherlands,* 1889.

H. M. Doughty. *Our Wherry in Wendish Lands,* 1891.

P. H. Emerson. *On English Lagoons,* 1893.

Walter Rye. *A Month on the Norfolk Broads on board the wherry Zoe and its tender, the tub Lotus,* 1887.

Glossary

Binns .... The deck edge which overhung the planking of the hull. Protected by the binn iron, an iron strip with a rounded outside face. Bends was a term used for the wales or rubbing strakes employed in shipbuilding in the seventeenth and eighteenth centuries, and the wherryman's term may be derived from this.

Boaked .... Wherrymen described a wherry as being boaked when it was laden so that the hatches were raised above their usual position. The body portion of a cart or barrow is the boke, a boke barrow being one fitted with sides, hence probably the wherryman's term.

Bunch of pears .... A decorative device which was drawn entirely with a pair of compasses. It was sometimes seen on the square section at the foot of the mast, sometimes on the masthead, when it was centred on the herring hole.

Carling hatch .... The hatchway in the foredeck through which the foot of the mast swings as the mast is lowered. So called, presumably, from the carling or carline, the fore-and-aft timber supporting the deck at the sides of a hatch. The small cover fitted to this hatch-way was known as the carling board.

Coburg .... A wooden wedge-shaped fairing which prevented the sheet blocks and sail from fouling the protruding part of the stove pipe; the wooden chimney fitted on top of this. The origin of the term is unknown, but it seems likely that it is connected in some way with Prince Albert of Saxe-Coburg, Consort of Queen Victoria, who also gave his title to a type of bread loaf, a dress fabric and a hat.

Crane iron .... The masthead fitting from which the upper halyard block was slung; not in fact a crane as fitted in some craft but an iron eyeband.

Crutch block .... The throat block, the halyard block hooked to the gaff near the jaws, which the wherrymen called the crutch.

Herring hole .... The slot in the masthead fitted with a sheeve over which the halyard is carried. Derivation is unknown; it has been suggested that it is connected with earing, but there seems to be no connection (Earing, ropes used to fasten the corners of the heads of sails to the yards, by the cringles. The upper corners of sails are frequently termed earings.—Dixon Kemp.)

Planksheer .... The outside plank at the deck edge which covers in the timber heads, and shows the sheer of the vessel. The same as covering board (Dixon Kemp). The wherry-man gave his own pronunciation, "plancher," to this perfectly normal if rather archaic boat-building term, which led to some odd spellings and to suggested derivations from the French.

Plankway .... The side deck, usually made from a single broad plank, on either side of the hold and cabin.

Quant .... Wooden pole having a turned wooden bott (button) at the head and a steel-shod toe, together with a wooden foot to prevent it sinking into the mud, used for propelling a wherry in calm or against the wind in narrow waters where tacking is impossible. Also used for giving the wherry a set off from the bank. A wherry's quant used to be 22 foot long, increased to 24 foot when the river was dredged to a greater depth.

Right-ups .... Hatch coamings. The use of this term seems to be peculiar to wherries.

Rond .... The low-lying section of river bank outside the raised river wall.

Rond anchor .... Stockless anchor with single fluke used on mooring lines when lying alongside the rond; unnecessary at staithes where mooring posts were provided.

Scandalised .... "A wherry is said to have her sail scandalised when it is half lowered, so as not to catch the wind, a slovenly way of getting out of reefing" (Walter Rye, 1895). Not entirely fair; the wherryman sometimes scandalised his sail by dropping the peak not to get out of reefing but to ease the strain when gybing.

Spans .... Wire or chain rigging used to distribute the weight of the gaff evenly throughout the length of the spar and so avoid a bending or breaking strain. The span block was the outer halyard block. Pronounced spen.

Spring stay .... The forestay. In other craft a spring stay is an extra stay set to prevent the mast from springing in a seaway.

Weather-cocked .... Wherrymen said a wherry was weather-cocked when on going about she lost way and could not fill her sail. After going astern a short distance she would pay off and the sail would fill.

INDEX

169

INDEX OF VESSELS (Trading wherries unless otherwise stated)

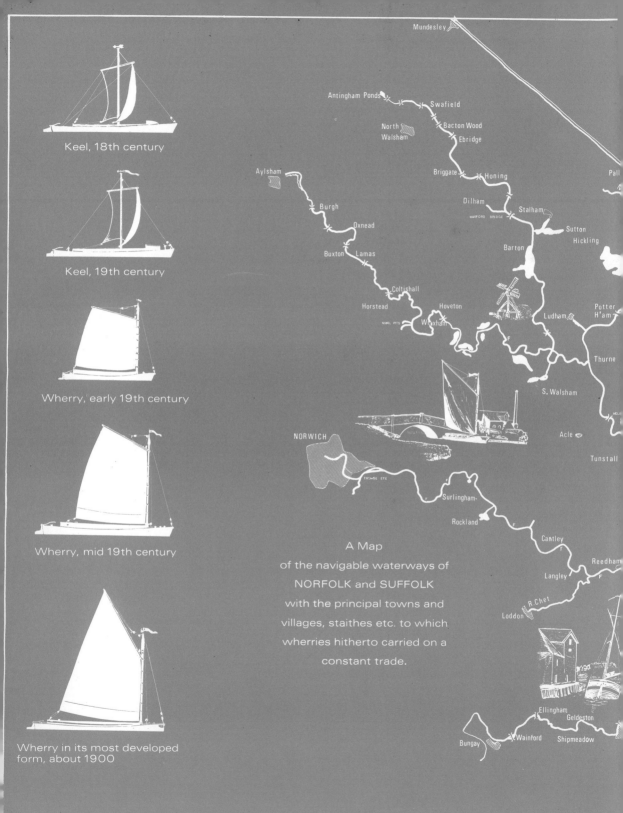

Keel, 18th century

Keel, 19th century

Wherry, early 19th century

Wherry, mid 19th century

Wherry in its most developed form, about 1900

A Map
of the navigable waterways of
NORFOLK and SUFFOLK
with the principal towns and
villages, staithes etc. to which
wherries hitherto carried on a
constant trade.

Mundesley

Antingham Ponds
Swafield
North Walsham
Bacton Wood
Ebridge
Aylsham
Briggate
Honing
Burgh
Dilham
Stalham
Oxnead
WAXHAM BRIDGE
Sutton
Hickling
Buxton
Lamas
Barton
Coltishall
Horstead
Hoveton
Potter H'am
MARL PITS
Wroxham
Ludham
Thurne
S. Walsham
Acle
NORWICH
Tunstall
TROWSE EYE
Surlingham
Rockland
Cantley
Reedham
Langley
R.Chet
Loddon
Ellingham
Geldeston
Bungay
Wainford
Shipmeadow

Pall